The Best Tips from
25 Years of *Fine Woodworking*

FINISHING

METHODS OF WORK

EDITED AND
ILLUSTRATED BY
JIM RICHEY

The Taunton Press

Publisher: Jim Childs
Associate Publisher: Helen Albert
Associate Editor: Strother Purdy
Copy Editor: Diane Sinitsky
Indexer: Harriet Hodges
Art Director: Paula Schlosser
Cover and Interior Designer: Carol Singer
Layout Artist: Kathe Donovan
Illustrator: Jim Richey

FINE WOODWORKING MAGAZINE
Editor: Timothy D. Schreiner
Art Director: Bob Goodfellow
Managing Editor: Anatole Burkin
Associate Editors: William Duckworth, Matthew Teague, Asa Christiana
Copy/Production Editor: Thomas McKenna
Associate Art Director: Michael Pekovich

ABOUT YOUR SAFETY
Working with wood is inherently dangerous. Using hand or power tools improperly or ignoring standard safety practices can lead to permanent injury or even death. Don't try to perform operations you learn about here (or elsewhere) unless you're certain they are safe for you. If something about an operation doesn't feel right, don't do it. Look for another way. We want you to enjoy the craft, so please keep safety foremost in your mind whenever you're working with wood.

Taunton
BOOKS & VIDEOS

for fellow enthusiasts

Printed in the United States of America
10 9 8 7 6 5 4 3 2 1

The Taunton Press, Inc.
63 South Main Street, PO Box 5506
Newtown, CT 06470-5506
e-mail: tp@taunton.com

Distributed by Publishers Group West

Library of Congress Cataloging-in-Publication Data
Finishing : methods of work / edited and illustrated by Jim Richey.
p. cm.
"The best tips from 25 years of Fine woodworking."
Includes index.
ISBN 1-56158-371-5
1. Wood finishing. I. Richey, Jim. II. Fine woodworking.
TT325.F5295 2000
684'.084—dc21 00-039255

FINISHING

METHODS OF WORK

ACKNOWLEDGMENTS

MAKING GOOD MAGAZINE COLUMNS and books is not a solitary endeavor—it requires collaboration of the finest kind. Twenty-some years ago John Kelsey took a chance on me—thanks, John. My deepest gratitude goes to the magazine staff members I've worked with over the years: Rick Mastelli, Jim Cummins, Jim Boesel, Alec Waters, and Bill Duckworth. These guys did most of the hard work and didn't get much of the credit. I'd like also to recognize art directors Roland Wolf and Bob Goodfellow for their gentle and perceptive coaching. I am also most grateful for Strother Purdy's help and support in putting together this series of books.

But most important, I would like to thank the hundreds of woodworkers whose creative ideas and clever tricks are represented here. We couldn't have done it without you.

CONTENTS

INTRODUCTION

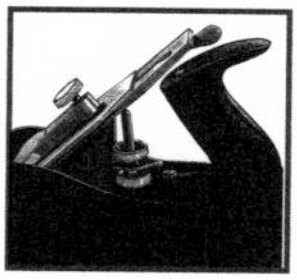

To some of us, and I'm including myself here, finishing is an afterthought. If you're in this camp you probably regard finishing as a sort of "mandatory obligation" you do after the real woodworking has been completed. Finishing is not only hard work (who among us really likes to sand?) but also rife with project-ruining risks.

Most of my frustration, I'll admit, comes from confusion over all the finishing choices. The shelves at even my small-town hardware store overflow with a whole family reunion of oils, lacquers, varnishes, and several cousins from the urethane family. There are pigmented stains, aniline dyes, and even strange organic products and chemicals that color the wood. I hate to admit it but I was in the penetrating-oil-finish rut for years. I used it on every project even though it sometimes gave the effect I wanted and sometimes didn't. But hey, it was simple.

This book sets out to remove a bit of the frustration that goes with finishing. I have selected the best finishing tips and techniques from 25 years of *Fine Woodworking* magazine's two informational columns, "Methods of Work" and "Q&A." Here you will find dozens of finishing recipes that were successful for real woodworkers. You'll learn how to prepare and stain wood, how to select the right finish, and how to apply it. There's an extra-long chapter on troubleshooting finishing problems. And who among us won't admit to having a finishing problem or two?

Maybe this book will just make you jump out of whatever finishing rut you're in.

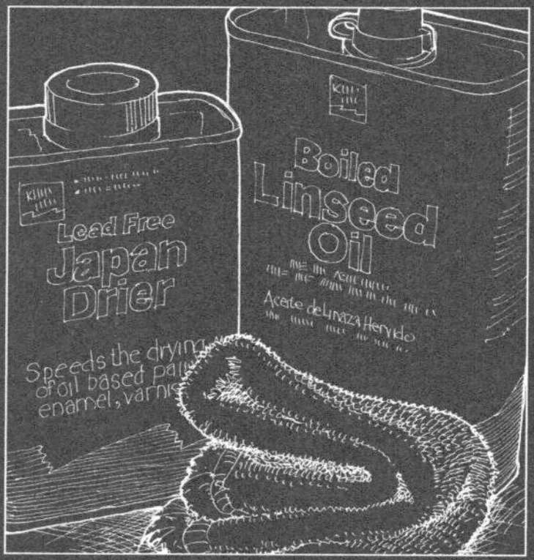
Lead Free
Japan
Drier
Speeds the drying
Boiled
Linseed
Oil
Aceite de Linaza Hervido

Chapter 1

SELECTING & APPLYING FINISHES

Choosing a Finish

As a finishing expert I'm often asked to identify the best and easiest finish for a woodworking project. The truth is there is no best finish, and easy depends on your finishing abilities. Like life, finishing is a series of compromises. Let's take, for example, a set of kitchen cabinets made from birch plywood. I think a solvent-based polyurethane varnish would be the appropriate finish. But don't just open the can and slap on the stuff. Most oil-based varnishes are too thick to flow and level well straight from the can. I always thin my varnish to about the consistency of whole milk before applying it to my project. (For the technically inclined, the actual flow rate is 13 seconds with a Zahn #3 viscosity cup, an inexpensive, easy-to-use accessory available at better paint supply houses.) The thinned varnish takes more coats to build a substantial film, but I've found it's easier to brush on a few extra coats than to sand off a thick one that has bumps, ridges, and bubbles.

The extended drying time of oil-based varnishes is both a blessing and a problem. Long drying times allow the finish to level evenly, but they tend to pick up dust in the process. The drying time can be shortened by adding Japan drier or, better yet, a small amount of cobalt drier to the thinned varnish. Be careful, though; too much cobalt drier can cause brittle finish films and even slow down the drying process. Follow package instructions, and then test your concoction on scrap wood to be sure. I usually add about 10 drops of artist's cobalt drier (available in art supply stores) to 1 qt. of thinned varnish. This mixture usually dries to the touch in about one hour.

Brush selection plays an important role in how the final finish looks. Cheap brushes are hard to use and produce a lousy-looking finish. Expect to pay about $15 for a high-quality natural-bristle brush, an investment well worth the money. With proper care, a good brush will last a lifetime and improve with age.

Unlike waterborne finishes, you need not worry about raising the grain before applying a solvent-based finish, but the first coat should be sanded to remove the stiffened wood fuzz before applying subsequent coats.

A properly applied polyurethane varnish finish will not look plastic-coated and will give your cabinets more than enough protection. By the way, the companion video to *The Woodfinishing Book* by Michael Dresdner, *The Woodfinishing Video* (available from The Taunton Press), is the best primer on brush applying a solvent-based varnish that I have seen.

—CHRIS MINICK, *Stillwater, Minn.,*
from a question by Paul Lasicki, Warwick, N.Y.

Mineral Oil as a Possible Finish

I DO NOT CONSIDER MINERAL OIL a wood finish. It offers little protection to the wood since it does not polymerize and would therefore be neither physically stable nor a barrier to moisture. If applied to raw wood, it would enter the cell structure, but changes in temperature and atmospheric pressure could result in its bleeding out on the surface.

I have used mineral oil as a vehicle for pumice and rottenstone in rubbing down varnish finishes. Unlike water, it will not swell the wood if the wood is incompletely protected by finish. It could also be used as a furniture polish, to occasionally revitalize surface appearance by temporarily restoring light-reflectiveness and serving as a lubricant, but for this I prefer lemon oil.

—R. BRUCE HOADLEY, *Amherst, Mass.,*
from a question by William Marsano, Toronto, Ont., Canada

Linseed Oil Finish

BOILED LINSEED OIL, with about 5% Japan drier added, will offer far greater protection to wood than mineral oil. The manner in which linseed oil is used has much to do with the final result. The oil-drier mixture should be applied generously and left 15 to 30 minutes on the wood, so it can penetrate well. Then, as much oil should be taken off as possible by rubbing the wood hard with rags. The oiled surface should be given ample time (at least a week) to dry. The microscopic film of oil that remains on the wood will go through a chemical change and will become hard and solid, like a fine coat of varnish. Repeat this five or six times and you build up a fine protective shield on your wood, which, because of the repeated rubbing, also becomes pleasantly smooth. True, linseed oil does not compete with Chanel No. 5 for a pleasant smell, but the smell goes away with proper drying and hardening. Mineral, or paraffin, oil will not harden, and I never use it as a protective coating. However, when French polishing I would never use anything else.

—GEORGE FRANK, *South Venice, Fla.,*
from a question by William Marsano, Toronto, Ont., Canada

Mix boiled linseed oil with 5% Japan drier.

Finishing a Clock with Hot Linseed Oil

I BUILD HALL AND WALL CLOCKS, and I use only walnut lumber. When I am finished with the case I don't fill the wood or stain it. I use only hot boiled linseed oil—nothing else. It makes a very beautiful finish. The grain seems to come to the surface in streaks of brown and some black; if there is a knot it turns black. For heating the oil I use an electric glue pot of 1-qt. size. I heat the oil to a point where it is too hot to put on with a rag, so I use a 1-in. nylon paintbrush. A brush also gets into the corners better than a rag. After the oil is applied, let it set until you see dry spots appear. This could take from 5 to 20 minutes, depending on room temperature and humidity. Then take a wool cloth or pad and rub the wood until the oil seems to disappear. What you are doing is forcing the oil into the wood. One or more coats can be applied. If one of my clocks is scratched or nicked, all it takes is a little sanding and a little hot oil and the scratch disappears.

—GEORGE ECKHART, *Kenosha, Wis.*

Oil Finish for Red Oak

APPLYING OIL FINISHES TO POROUS woods like red oak requires some care. The oil can seep back out of the pores to create an uneven finish. Here's the technique I use to get good results. For starters you can only get a good-to-excellent finish by working hard to prepare the surfaces before applying the finish. Scrape the surface to remove any trace of machine marks, then sand with a cork sanding block and 120-grit sandpaper. Always sand in the direction of the grain. Continue the sanding with finer and finer grades until you have a very smooth surface with 220 grit. Naturally, it's important to remove all the sanding dust. I find vacuuming to be the best method.

Next, dip a rag in water and wring it out so it's damp, not wet, and wipe the wood surface. This will raise the wood grain. After the surface has dried thoroughly, sand again with 220-grit paper. Some people skip the wetting step, saying the first coat of oil will also raise the grain, but I think surfaces treated with water dry faster and are easier to sand.

After cleaning the surface thoroughly, apply a thin coat of finish with a rag or brush. I'd recommend thinning the oil 50/50 with mineral spirits or, better yet, turpentine. Let the first thin coat dry until tacky, then wipe off the excess. Let the finish dry 24 hours before applying a second coat, this time with undiluted oil. Some finishers use 400-grit wet/dry silicon-carbide paper to apply the second coat, but that's a matter of individual preference. The important thing to remember is that the finish must be applied in light coats. If you put on heavy coats, the excess will ooze out of the pores for days.

Normally only two coats are required, but you may want to apply a third after the second coat dries for a week.

—OTTO HEUER, *Waukegan, Ill.,*
from a question by Kent Korgenski, Salt Lake City, Utah

Finishing a Walnut Grandfather Clock

HERE'S THE BEST WAY I'VE FOUND to oil-finish a walnut grandfather clock to bring out the wood's color, texture, and grain. First prepare the surface by removing all visible planer marks, saw marks, and other blemishes with 60-grit garnet paper, always sanding with the grain. When the marks are gone, keep sanding for the same length of time again, still using 60-grit paper.

Now, using 80-grit paper, sand for a single period of time (call it a cycle) to remove the deepest scratches left by the 60-grit paper. Follow with 120-grit open-coat finishing paper for two cycles. Do not use finer grit paper at this time.

Brush on a generous coat of boiled linseed oil. Allow it to dry for four to six hours, until a thin film or skin begins to form over the surface. The timing is crucial. Then rub vigorously with a coarsely woven cloth until the surface appears dry. Allow it to sit overnight, and then sand for one cycle with 220-grit finishing paper. An oily substance will build up on the paper, by which time the oil will have served its purpose.

Repeat with as many applications of oil, fine-sanding between each, as is necessary to achieve the desired gloss. Apply the last two coats without sanding. This process can produce a beautiful finish, but depending on the kind of use it will receive, some maintenance may be required in the form of later applications of oil.

—ANDY MARLOW, *from a question by Robert Stewart, Eddystone, Pa.*

Two Finishes for Carvings

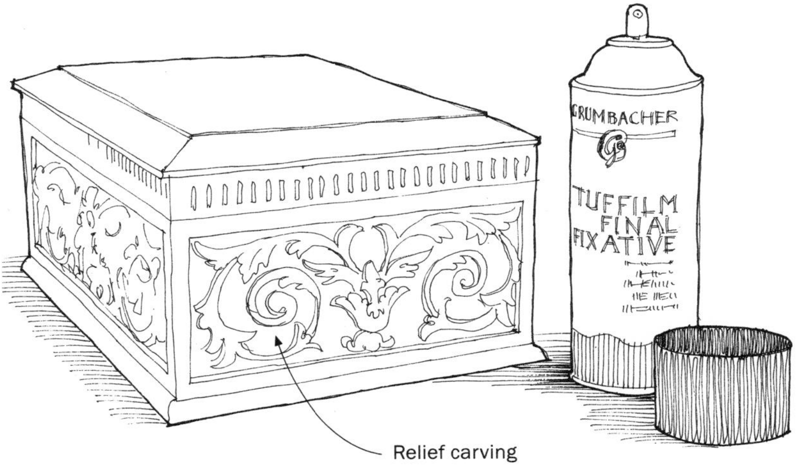

HERE ARE TWO OIL FINISHES for relief carvings that will let you achieve that hand-rubbed look. For low relief carvings, I prefer a very traditional finish. Pour a pint of boiled linseed oil into a double boiler (a small saucepan sitting in a larger pan that contains about an inch of water), add ¼ pint of turpentine, and season to taste with a few healthy shavings from a bar of beeswax. Heat this on a stove over medium-low heat and stir until the wax is totally melted into the mixture. Remove from the burner and let cool until warm and then pour it into a jar with a tight lid. (Note: Because of the possible fire danger, perform this technique very carefully, preferably on an electric hot plate set up outdoors in a fire-safe area and never over an open flame.)

When you're ready to use your oil mixture, shake the jar vigorously and then brush a medium coat of the oil on the wood (you don't have to reheat the mixture). Let this set up for 10 to 15 minutes and then buff with a soft, lint-free cloth. You should get a nice satin sheen.

The second finish is virtually fail-proof for both high and low relief work. Brush boiled linseed oil on the carving and wipe off the excess immediately with a lint-free cloth or soft paper towels. Make sure the damp linseed oil is completely wiped off. Let the carving sit for about an hour and then lay it flat and spray on a medium coat of Grumbacher's "Tuffilm" matte spray (available from art supply stores). Let it dry for five minutes and then spray another coat. Spray once more and then let it set up for a few hours.

The surface will feel slightly rough when the Tuffilm has dried completely. Take a small piece of 0000 steel wool and gently rub the carving, making small twists in the steel wool to get into the carving's crevices. Fortunately, the places you can't reach with the steel wool still come out looking as smooth as the prominent surfaces on the carving. With a soft brush whisk away all of the steel-wool particles and then spray one more coat of the Tuffilm. Let it set up again for a few hours, then lightly steel-wool it again. You will have a nice satin finish. I've found Tuffilm is the most dependable spray finish for carvings on the market; the finishes are consistent and always even.

—John Heatwole, *Bridgewater, Va., from a question by Leslie McGregor, Elkhart, Ind.*

Tough, Easily Renewable Finish for a Tabletop

In my experience the best finish for a family table is a varnish/linseed oil finish. First, it is a relatively easy finish to use for large surfaces, and it can be rubbed out smooth. It's also easily renewable, which is very important for a table that's going to see some wear and tear. Finally, the finish will have a nice shine, but it won't look glossy or plastic. In fact, I am writing this sitting at a cherry table with just such a finish. The table has withstood beautifully the ravages of daily meals with three children and everything from gluing projects to watercolors.

Spray finishes such as lacquer also offer a good shine and provide more protection, but I am less familiar with them. On the down side, they require not only spray equipment but, even more important, a nearly pristine shop area in which to spray. My small shop just doesn't have the space.

Start by preparing the top surface really well (by that I mean evenly sanded to at least 220-grit or planed and scraped). The better the preparation, the more clarity and smoothness to the final finish. The finish mixture is made up from spar varnish (available from hardware and paint stores or marine-supply dealers), boiled linseed oil, and turpentine in roughly equal parts. You might want to thin the initial coat to get better surface penetration and to get a feel for the finishing process. Polyurethane varnishes and products that contain both urethanes and spar varnishes seem to work equally well, but I prefer spar for its high solids content and moderate odor.

I brush on the finish so that the surface appears wet, let it soak in and tack up, and then I rub it thoroughly with a clean, dry cloth to remove any excess. How long it takes to tack up depends on the temperature, humidity, and the proportion of varnish in the mix, but it should be something like 20 to 30 minutes. The first coat usually does not feel all that tacky because most of the finish soaks into the wood. It is really important to rub the excess off completely though, or you'll have a sticky mess that's a pain to remove.

With an open-grained wood such as ash, the grain often is filled before any finish is applied. I find this step can be eliminated though. Lightly sanding the wet finish with 220-grit (or finer) sandpaper smooths the surface and creates a pore-filling slurry. I would avoid wet-or-dry sandpaper on a light wood like ash because the silicon-carbide abrasive is dark and would inevitably lodge in the pores.

The finish will tack up more quickly with each coat and will require more rubbing to remove the excess. For a table that is going to see hard use, I recommend at least four coats, but a couple more wouldn't hurt. Additional coats only add to the depth and the beauty of the finish. For the topcoat, apply a mixture of beeswax, boiled linseed oil, and turpentine, melted together in a double boiler but not over an open flame. Be careful—the mixture is extremely flammable. I apply this last coat with 0000 steel wool.

To rejuvenate the finish if it ever looks dull, clean the surface with a little turpentine and linseed oil on 0000 steel wool, and then apply a coat of the varnish mixture followed by a coat of paste wax.

—GARRETT HACK, *Thetford Center, Vt.,*
from a question by Clifton Myll, La Quinta, Calif.

Mix boiled linseed oil, spar varnish, and turpentine in equal parts.

Oil and Shellac Finish

NORMALLY YOU WOULDN'T MIX OIL and shellac, which are completely different finishes. If done right, however, an oil and shellac finish gives fast and beautiful results. I first used the finish about 30 years ago to repair the side of a cabinet that had gotten badly scratched as it was being unloaded from a truck. Because it would have taken me about three days to restore the original oil finish, I decided to take a chance on an untried method. Once I had scraped and sanded the damaged side, I applied some oil and followed it with an application of shellac. When the surface had dried thoroughly, I rubbed it down with steel wool, and it came out as beautiful as the rest of the cabinet.

When I first demonstrated the method to my woodworking students, they named it the "four-F" finish (Frid's fast fine finish). Before trying the finish yourself, make sure to get the right ingredients—raw (not boiled) linseed oil or Watco oil, and orange (not white) shellac. Don't mix the oil with the shellac, but apply the oil evenly and sparingly to the prepared surface with a rag. Then immediately brush on a three-pound cut of orange shellac, leave it until it gets tacky, and then rub the surface with a pad of 000 steel wool. Next wipe it clean with a clean, dry cloth, taking care to remove all of the oil and shellac from the surface. If any excess remains, the finish will turn gray. If necessary, another coat can be applied a short while later, but this time using less oil.

This finish is best for small pieces and things like chairs and table bases because it is not waterproof. If water is left on it for a while and it spots, you can repair it easily. Put oil on the spot, steel-wool or sand until the spot disappears, and wipe off all the excess.

—TAGE FRID

Filling the Pores in French Polishing

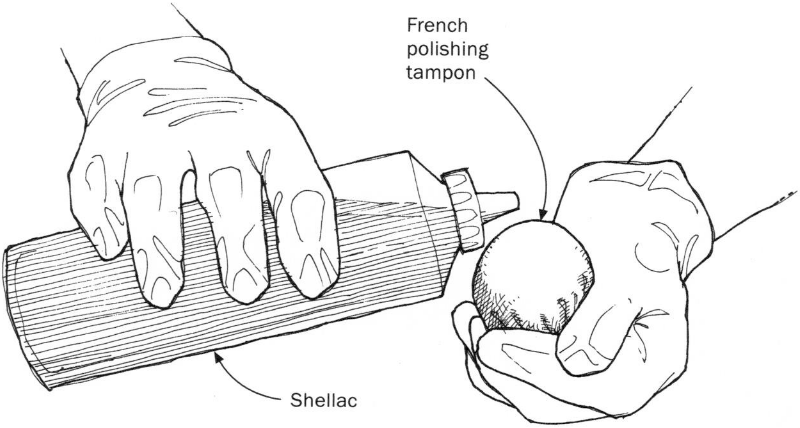

ONE COMMON QUESTION I get from woodworkers just learning how to apply a French polish is "what filler should I use to fill the pores of the wood?" For real French polishing, you would use no filler. Part of French polishing is to work pumice stone into the surface of the wood with a special pad that the English call a "rubber," the French a "tampon." The tampon's heart is wool from old socks or sweaters. It is about the size and shape of an egg, and will fit the inside of your palm, where you hold it quite firmly. The wool's role is to hold and slowly release the alcohol and later the liquid shellac. The wool is wrapped in a porous fabric—linen is best—which covers it snugly and smoothly on the bottom. This bottom side becomes quite flat, since it will slide and slide on the surface of the wood.

You feed the wool with a few drops of alcohol at a time and sprinkle some finely ground pumice stone on the surface to be polished. Then, with broad circling motions, you begin to force the pumice into the pores. The pumice first will fill up the small spaces of the linen, and being abrasive, it will cut off invisibly small particles of the wood. Together these will slowly fill the pores under the pressured rubbing of your fists. Since the pumice carries with itself the finest possible wood dust, it takes on the color of the wood and thus becomes invisible.

However, not all French polishers go through this slow and tiring process. Many use various kinds of fillers. Once common recipe: Powdered chalk or simple whiting powder is the filling agent, colored with dry powdered colors to match the wood. The binder is rosin (or colophony), also powdered, and the carrier is mineral spirits. The spirits are frequently tinted (for dark walnut) with some asphaltum paint. The amount of rosin is about 10% to 15% of the colored chalk. Another recipe is talcum powder colored with dry pigment. The carrier and the binder are shellac and alcohol. This type of filler is difficult to use without skill and experience.

Another approach, which ignores filling the pores altogether, is called open-pore French polishing. It was practiced widely in the first 20 years of this century. First the wood is sanded impeccably, then the dust is brushed or blown off, leaving all the pores open. The tampon is moistened with a few drops of shellac, further cut with a little alcohol. Again the rubbing begins, except that this time the tampon works with the grain, each passage leaving a breath of shellac on the wood. Repeat until a pleasant shine appears. No pumice is used, no attempt is made to fill the pores, and no oil is used either. The tampon should never be too moist, and each film must dry before the next one is applied. This type of French polishing does not have the bright glossy shine of the filled version, but it is far easier to obtain and still quite pleasant to look at.

—GEORGE FRANK, *South Venice, Fla.,*
from a question by E. Thomas Akyali, New York, N.Y.

Tung Oil Finish for Gunstocks

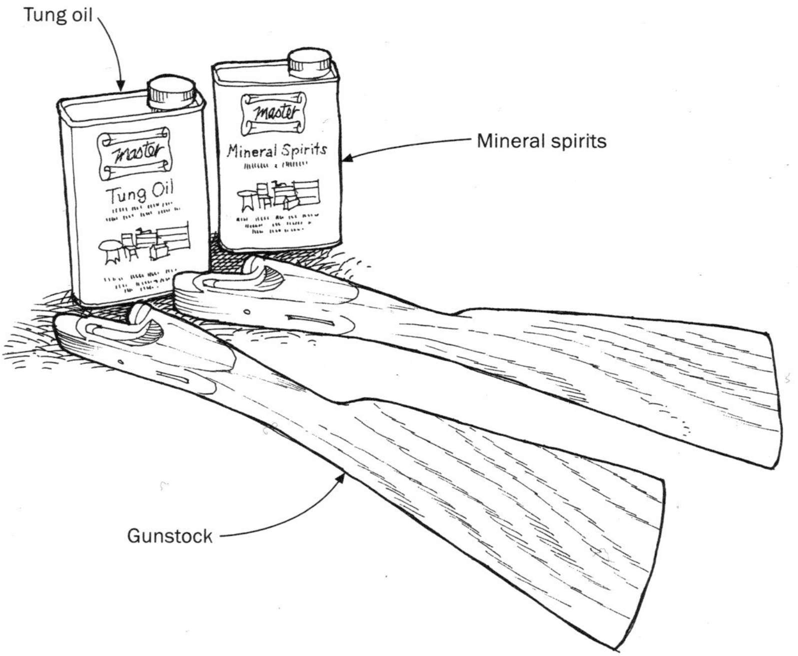

IN MY OPINION TUNG OIL is the best finish for a gun you use in the field. It is a better moisture shield than other drying oils and is probably better than the commercial varnishes and penetrating oils for the same reason. You can use pure tung oil (sold by Sutherland Welles, 403 Weaver St., Carrboro, NC 27570 and by Woodcraft Supply, 560 Airport Industrial Park, P.O. Box 1686, Parkersburg, WV 26102) or polymerized tung oil, which Welles also sells. The pure tung oil dries to a dull finish, and I prefer polymerized tung, which gives you a much higher sheen. You get a decent gloss, especially if you apply several coats thinly, well rubbed in by hand.

Thin down the first coat of tung with mineral spirits. Use about 75% oil to 25% thinner by volume so that it penetrates deeply. Apply it fairly wet, particularly on end grain at the butt, at the fore-end tip, and the pistol grip. Soak the inside of the inletting. Where end grain soaks it up quickly, apply until no more soaks in. Then wipe it all down and let it sit for 48 hours. Don't let it build up on the surface during this first seal coat or you'll get uneven gloss later.

After it's dried for a couple of days, start rubbing in by hand a thin coat of the oil, unthinned. Let it dry 24 hours and repeat. What you're doing now is building up a thin layer on the top of the wood. One seal coat followed by two thin coats should be all you need to achieve a moisture-resistant, durable finish that resists abrasion, handling, and perspiration.

Watco Danish Oil should work well also, as should Waterlox Transparent Seal, Minwax Antique Oil, McCloskey's Tungseal Danish Oil, and ZAR Wipe-On Tung finish. They all are excellent products and should do what you want if you treat them as penetrating-type finishes and not as surface varnishes. This means using a thinned-down first coat followed by a well-rubbed second coat. Don't let the oil build up in the checkered areas. You'll never get it off once it dries.

Avoid using water-based finishing products on gunstocks, since they will introduce water into the wood. This is a good way to warp the forearm and change the point of aim, as the warped wood will bear against the barrel.

—DON NEWELL, *Farmington, Mich.,*
from a question by Ralph Gustin, Brookings, S.D.

Two Beeswax & Linseed Oil Finishes

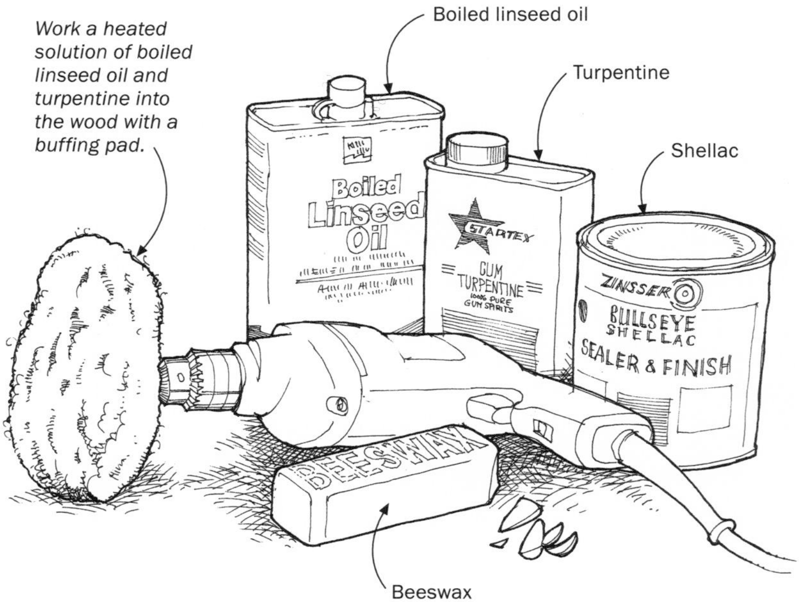

I WOULD LIKE TO PASS ON a beeswax and linseed oil finish that was given to me by a friend. This finish is excellent for walnut and cherry because it enhances the natural grain and coloring without "hiding" the wood. I begin by flowing a heated solution of ⅔ boiled linseed oil and ⅓ turpentine on the wood. I work this into the wood with a buffing pad on my electric drill, pressing hard to build heat from friction. After letting this dry for a day, I seal and fill the grain with a coat of orange shellac, allow to dry, and rub off with 000 steel wool. At this point, I make a mixture of beeswax and boiled linseed oil in a can on my wife's candlemaking stove. I apply this mixture hot to the wood and rub it with a rag. After wiping off the excess and letting it set for a few days, I take any smeariness off with a little Johnson's Pledge. This finish is easy to do and gives me a deep, lustrous sheen that resists marking. In the event of damage, I have found that it patches very easily by simply sanding an area through to the wood and applying the process again.

—MYRON J. ZWIZANSKI, *West Chester, Pa.*

HERE'S AN OLD FINISH RECIPE that is quite effective. It calls for one part melted beeswax, one part boiled linseed oil, and one part turpentine. These three ingredients are heated together until liquid, then applied while hot. After a few minutes any excess finish is buffed off. You can vary the ingredients a bit without altering the result much. For instance, excess beeswax will increase drying time, though not as much as excess linseed oil. Excess turpentine will increase the speed of drying.

The merit of this finish is that once warmed, it will go into the surface of the wood and into the open grain of oak particularly well. The colder wood will soon harden the mixture so it can be polished with a rag or a soft brush, which works well on carvings or molding.

—IAN J. KIRBY, *N. Bennington, Vt., from a question by Jim Smith, St. Louis, Mo.*

Making a Wax Mixture

BY MIXING VARIOUS KINDS OF WAXES you can create your own custom furniture polish with the characteristics you desire. Start with beeswax, which has been used on furniture for centuries, both as a primary finish and as a polish. Mix beeswax with hard waxes such as carnauba or candelilla to produce the polish. I'd recommend against using paraffin wax, a petroleum derivative; it is usually added to polishes more to reduce the cost than to improve the quality.

Any wax can be made into a paste by mixing the wax with a solvent, such as turpentine or mineral spirits, and heating it in a double boiler. However, if done on a stove top, this is a highly dangerous operation that can easily result in a fire or explosion, so I don't advocate amateurs doing it. Fortunately, there is another method that is quite a bit slower than the heating method but far safer. First, shred the wax into a lidded glass or metal container. Add about ½ pint of solvent to 1 lb. of wax and stir the solution to an even consistency. Then, simply shake or stir the mixture from time to time for several days until all the wax is dissolved. If you want the paste to be thicker or thinner, either add a little more wax or more solvent. Rottenstone, oil-based pigments or dark-color dyes can be added to create different antique and scratch-covering effects.

—BOB FLEXNER, *Norman, Okla.,*
from a question by William H. Crist, Charleston, W.Va.

Sheraton's Wax Finishing Process for Antiques

SHERATON, THE ENGLISH FURNITURE DESIGNER, explained his finishing process thus: Procure fine red-brick dust (for color and grain filler). Add a mixture of beeswax dissolved in turpentine to use as a rubbing paste. The first coat is applied with a cloth, allowing one to two hours drying time. Rub vigorously with the same cloth; finish rubbing with the grain. Allow two days drying time between coats. Repeat with a second coat. When the brick dust seems to have served its purpose, continue wax and turpentine only. The more you work on it, the better it will look. This finish will need occasional maintenance. For the glue joints, have your glue thinned sufficiently so that none shows between joined surfaces, and clamp tightly. A hairline will always show unless grain structure matches fairly well.

—ANDY MARLOW

Renewing Paste Wax

I'VE NOTICED THAT WOODWORKERS who apply a heavy paste-wax layer over a penetrating oil finish are often disappointed later when the wax loses its sheen. A paste-wax sheen fades either because the wax layer is too heavy and turns yellow or because it's too thin and gets wiped away. It's not good to build up a thick coating of wax on wood, and it should be removed every so often. Just wet the wood with mineral spirits or paint thinner (not lacquer thinner, which will dissolve the finish) and scrub the wetted surfaces with 000 steel wool. Turn the pad often and rinse it in the solvent when it gets clogged with wax. It will take two or three such washings to get the surface clean.

Once you get the wax off, I advise against reapplying it. Instead, rub in by hand another coat of your penetrating oil finish, thinned down a trifle with mineral spirits. When this has dried for about 45 minutes, buff the surface vigorously with a lint-free wad of cotton cloth (an old bath towel) or with a lamb's-wool bonnet chucked in your electric drill. This will give you a good sheen without a shine and will be a durable finish.

—DON NEWELL, *Farmington, Mich., from a question by Ralph A. Bove, Jr., Asbury Park, N.J.*

Lacquer over Oil

OIL UNDER SPRAYED NITROCELLULOSE lacquer is one of my favorite finishes for walnut and cherry. Oil brings out a wood's figure and color, and the lacquer protects it from damage. Start with a Danish oil finish like Watco or Deftoil. Danish oil finishes are really long-oil varnishes, which means they dry harder and, more important, cure quickly. Typically, I allow the Danish oil to dry for three or four days. Then I lightly scuff-sand the wood and apply a nitrocellulose lacquer topcoat. I have used this system for years and have not seen any adhesion problems in the lacquer.

You may be tempted to use linseed oil as the base coat. I'd recommend against it. Linseed oil takes a surprisingly long time to cure. Seven to 10 days is not uncommon, especially if your shop is on the cool side or if there is a lot of oil in the wood. Topcoating the oiled wood before the oil has completely cured will lead to adhesion problems.

—CHRIS MINICK, *Stillwater, Minn., from a question by Charles Amen, Streamwood, Ill.*

Homemade Beeswax Mixtures

BEESWAX IS A WONDERFUL SUBSTANCE. It can be used as a furniture polish, a wood preservative, and it also makes a good wood lubricant. Due to its chemical makeup, beeswax is totally insoluble in water and alcohol and only slightly soluble in other common household solvents. Therefore, beeswax makes a very good furniture polish; it's used extensively in paste-wax polishes. Commercial beeswax-based furniture polishes contain mineral spirits or turpentine as solvents for the wax, and you can use the same solvents to dissolve raw beeswax from beehives.

A good furniture polish can be made by adding 1¼ cup of mineral spirits or turpentine to 1 lb. of melted beeswax. Either solvent is highly explosive, and the mixture should under no circumstances be heated over an open flame. After the mixture has cooled, it will have the consistency of shoe polish. More or less solvent can be added to change the consistency of the paste. Beeswax polish is an excellent finish for wooden cooking utensils and cutting boards because beeswax is nontoxic; it's even accepted by the Food and Drug Administration as a food additive.

A waterproofer for exterior wood can be made by mixing mineral spirits, beeswax, and boiled linseed oil in the following ratio: 1 gal. of mineral spirits; 1 oz. to 2 oz. of beeswax; and 1½ cups of boiled linseed oil. This waterproofer should be used on bare wood only, and two to three coats are needed to achieve optimum waterproofing. Additional coats of the same mixture should be applied every two years.

Finally, the chemical structure of beeswax can be used as a lubricant for wood. A thin coating of beeswax on a sticking drawer will make the drawer slide much easier.

—CHRIS MINICK, *Stillwater, Minn.,*
from a question by Denis, Louisa, Va.

Beeswax: Excellent Polish, Poor Finish

OFTEN WOODWORKERS will apply a beeswax finish to bare wood expecting an attractive, waterproof, renewable finish. Although it is true that beeswax is insoluble in water, it is not true that beeswax is impermeable to water and therefore it alone will not provide sufficient protection to unfinished wood on a surface such as a countertop. The beeswax film allows moisture to penetrate and swell the wood fibers, creating the appearance of light-colored spots or streaks. The beeswax formulation is a polish formulation intended to be used on pre-finished wood pieces. The function of a polish is quite different from that of a finish. A polish is used to enhance the beauty of the finish, to serve as a renewable sacrificial coating, and to provide a slick surface to deflect blows and prevent them from scratching the finish.

Fortunately, an easy, nontoxic solution to the problem exists. First, sand the countertop with 180-grit sandpaper to remove the existing beeswax. Wet the surface with water to raise the grain and sand flat after it has dried. Once the grain has been raised and sanded smooth, future grain-raising problems are minimized. Now apply two sealer coats of shellac diluted to about a two-pound cut. It is better to prepare your own shellac sealer from dry shellac flakes. Lightly sand the sealer coats with 220-grit sandpaper to ensure a smooth finish. Finally, apply two or three coats of beeswax polish, and buff to the desired gloss level. If you prefer, a carnauba wax-based furniture polish will also produce acceptable results. This finishing combination, sealer plus wax, should provide the needed water resistance for your countertop. And periodic reapplication of the wax will keep it looking good.

—CHRIS MINICK, *Stillwater, Minn.,*
from a question by E. G. Steidemann, Madison, Wisc.

Two Alcohol-Resistant Bartop Finishes

IF YOU WANT TO CREATE an alcohol-resistant bartop finish, I'd suggest a good alcohol-proof lacquer or varnish that can be dulled to an oil flatness with steel wool. Contrary to what many believe, you don't have to build up many coats to protect the wood. Two coats of lacquer or varnish should offer excellent protection in most cases.

—GEORGE FRANK, *from a question by Alexius R. Robben, San Antonio, Tex.*

FOR AN ALCOHOL-RESISTANT OIL FINISH, I would apply a mixture of equal parts of tung oil, Japan drier, and mineral spirits, and let this dry 32 to 48 hours. Sand lightly and apply a second coat, allowing it to dry about 36 hours. Carefully dispose of any rags used with this mixture, as it may produce spontaneous combustion, or else store them in a fireproof container. Alcohol resistance can come from a product such as Varathane, made by Fletco International (100002 45 St., Oakland, CA 94608). Thin this finish with two parts of the proper reducer to one part of the varnish, and brush on a thin coat. A mixture of two parts tung oil, two parts mineral spirits, and one part phenolic spar varnish might work as well. Apply two coats at 36-hour intervals, sanding lightly between coats.

—OTTO HEUER, *Waukegan, Ill., from a question by Alexius R. Robben, San Antonio, Tex.*

Satin Piano Finish

I RECENTLY HELPED SOLVE A PROBLEM in our shop that specializes in spraying ebony piano finishes. We use a black nitrocellulose lacquer and were having no problems until the final rubout. In our original process, we wet-sanded the lacquer with a pneumatic straight-line sander and 400-grit paper lubricated with mineral spirits. We then rubbed the piano with 0000 steel wool that is unraveled and stretched across a short, narrow board with a felt pad tacked to it so the steel wool stays flat against the finish. The rubout resulted in an even-looking satin finish, but instead of deep black, the finish had a gray look, most noticeable toward the edges of the lids. We tried all kinds of rubbing compounds and oils, to no avail. Some even highlighted the sandpaper scratches.

In frustration, I visited a piano dealer to see what kind of finishes factories produce on new pianos. When I examined the satin-ebony grands by Steinway and by Yamaha, I noticed that the "gray look" is common to both. I believe it is caused by light bouncing off the minute scratches left by both the abrasive paper and the steel wool.

I noticed that the scratches on the Yamaha are almost perfectly straight, parallel, and uninterrupted. Then I learned that the final rubout on a Yamaha piano is done by machine, with the entire lid passing on a belt under a roller that rubs out the full width in one pass. The Steinway finish looks more like ours because it's rubbed out by hand. We finally deduced that the extra refraction near the edges happens when you reverse direction as you rub. Obviously, the individual particles on the abrasive paper or the individual strands of steel wool don't stay exactly in the same grooves. Instead, tiny "hooks" are created near the edge of the lid at the point of reversal.

Our solution was to rub the lacquer with silicon carbide paper only. We changed the sanding lubricant to a mix of paraffin oil and mineral spirits. This lubricant removes more lacquer than steel wool, so we apply additional coats before sanding.

We wet-sand with 400 grit until the surface is smooth, flat, and uniform. Then we wet-sand with 600 grit at right angles to the 400-grit scratches until these are gone—a process called cross-sanding. Next, we wet-sand with 1,200 grit at right angles to the 600-grit scratches until they disappear (we special-order 3M "ultra-fine" paper in grits from 1,200 to 1,500 through an automotive-paint supply house). Voila! We now have a superior satin finish.

—DONALD STEINERT, *Grants Pass, Ore., from a question by John Minor, Champaign, Ill.*

Lacquer Finish on Rosewood

EXOTIC WOODS LIKE COCOBOLO and rosewood are high in natural oils, which leads to such finishing problems as slow drying, crazing, clouding, lacquer checking, "peanut-shell" adhesion, and bleeding. The C. F. Martin Company, whose guitars incorporate exotic woods, has developed a solution to these problems. Years of experimentation (and experience) have led to a lacquer finish that is thin, flexible, and durable—actually improving the tone of the instrument with age.

Sherwin-Williams Co. formulates finish products to meet our specific production needs. They also sell equivalent products in their retail stores, so I'll list the stock number for the standard retail item.

First, your finishing room must be dust-free and well ventilated. To prepare for finishing, sand the surfaces with 180-grit paper and then scrape along the grain, removing any scratches left by sanding. Now spray on a coat of vinyl washcoat (Sherwin-Williams #T69-F2). The vinyl washcoat, the key ingredient in the process, seals in the wood's natural oils and serves as a base for the wood filler. After this application cures for at least two hours, abrade the surfaces lightly with a scuff pad or sand lightly with 400-grit aluminum-oxide paper. Now the wood is ready for filling.

Martin uses a silica-based filler (Sherwin-Williams #D70-T1), which thins with naphtha and mineral spirits. We use it on all porous woods (rosewood, mahogany, cocobolo, zebrawood, and others) to provide a uniform base for the lacquer. This filler is syrupy, and you apply it with a brush. It gets leathery after about five minutes, at which point you rub it into the pores of the wood with a cotton rag tied into a bun. Then carefully remove the excess.

Apply another full coat of vinyl washcoat to the top and, when it cures, sand it lightly with 400-grit paper. Spray a final coat of vinyl washcoat over the entire body and let it cure for at least two hours. Then spray on a coat of lacquer sealer (Sherwin-Williams #T60-F10), which must cure for a minimum of 30 minutes (sand the surface if it sits overnight) before the first coat of gloss lacquer is applied. The same day, spray on two or three wet coats of gloss lacquer (Sherwin-Williams #T77-F12), allowing 45 minutes drying time between each coat. Sand the surfaces lightly the next day with silicon carbide paper (280 grit), taking care not to sand through the lacquer into the sealer coats. Apply another two or three coats of gloss lacquer, depending on the coarseness of the grain, waiting 45 minutes between. Sand again the next day, and apply two more full coats, making six coats in all. Leave the final coat unsanded.

To get a flat finish, spray the final coat using a 50/50 mix of gloss and flat lacquer (Sherwin-Williams #T77-F13) and leave it unbuffed. Gloss surfaces should be buffed with a lamb's-wool bonnet and buffing compound (3-M #A5955) thinned with water. Buffing removes the "orange peel" (minute dimples) and yields a highly polished surface. A final buffing at a high RPM removes all the scratches left by the compound and completes the finish.

—DICK BOAK, *Martin Guitar Co., Nazareth, Pa.*

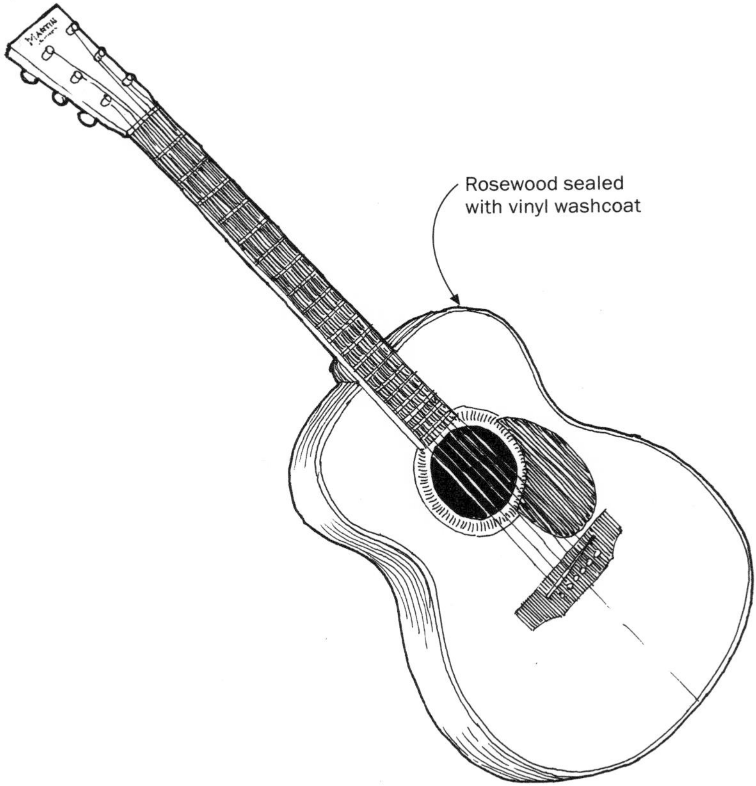

Finishing Oily Woods with Lacquer— A Simpler Approach

I CAN CONFIRM THAT DICK BOAK'S method (see pp. 31-33) for finishing oily woods with lacquer works quite well. But some readers might be interested in simpler alternatives.

If a lacquer finish, such as the one used by Martin Guitar, is desired, the vinyl-seal step and perhaps even the lacquer-seal step can be avoided by spraying on several light coats of shellac (3-lb. cut or less). Don't brush it on because this can cause blotchy running of the pigment from the pores of the wood, as the denatured alcohol used to thin the shellac also dissolves the pigment. Filler may also be dispensed with as the buildup of shellac and subsequent lacquer coats will eliminate all but the tiniest indications of the pores below the surface.

Two other finishes are possible. One is to apply a wet coat of Waterlox (a tung and linseed mix) and then wipe it off before it begins to set up. Let dry for 24 hours and repeat, after first sanding lightly with 320-grit paper. Wet-sand the final coat (it could take three or more) with mineral oil as a lubricant, and then wipe clean. When dry, apply a coat of wax. Finally, you could use Watco Teak Oil, which is manufactured specifically for finishing rosewood, teak, and other resinous woods.

The lacquer gives a spectacular finish but is easily scratched. On most furniture, scratches can be repaired by rubbing with 0000 steel wool. The successive-coat finish (Waterlox) has a more in-the-wood look and is more scratch resistant, but does not show off the figure and color of the wood as well as the lacquer finish. Watco Teak Oil seems to dissolve and disperse the pigment, darkening the whole appearance and reducing the vibrancy of the wood's color and figure.

—JOSHUA MARKEL, *Philadelphia, Pa.*

Oil on Lacquer Finish for Teak

TEAK IS A BEAUTIFUL BUT NOTORIOUSLY hard-to-finish wood because of its high oil content. Here's how Danish furniture makers do it. The first step must remove the natural, nondrying oil so it won't interfere with the drying of the finish or with its adhesion. Either of two solvents will work well. Use chlorothene or 1, 1, 1 trichlorothane (which is the same as chlorothene) or the cheapest lacquer thinner you can buy. Cheap thinner will dissolve anything on the wood, yet will evaporate off quickly and completely. Richer, more costly lacquer thinners have components that slow evaporation and can remain down in the wood, creating drying problems. Don't bother to try alcohol to remove the oil because it won't do a thing for you.

Swab a good, wet coat of solvent on the wood, let it set for a couple of minutes, and wipe dry with paper towels. The solvent will bring the oil up to the surface and the paper towels will absorb it. If you have a really oily piece of wood, cover the wetted areas with aluminum foil to retard solvent evaporation and let it soak for five to ten minutes, then wipe dry.

This should take out all the oil down to at least 1⁄16 in., which is plenty, since the finish will never penetrate this far. Any oil left down in the heart of the wood will be no trouble.

Now that the wood is oil-free, you're ready to proceed with the finish. Unless you have really light, figure-free wood, you probably won't have to stain—fine, since the more natural you leave the wood, the more natural it appears. To approximate an "oil treated on lacquer" finish, use a well-thinned lacquer to seal the wood, either one or two coats simply brushed, swabbed, or sprayed on. The lacquer seal will keep the final finish material from soaking into the wood too deeply. Once the lacquer seal has dried, rub in perhaps two coats of the final finish, with adequate drying time between. The final finish should be something like Watco Danish oil, which works like an oil but gives a good, durable finish. Two rubbed coats will give you the appearance you want without building up a film in the grain of the wood.

—DON NEWELL, *Farmington, Mich.,*
from a question by Roman Sorokin, Falls Church, Va.

Colorless Finish for Wooden Bowls?

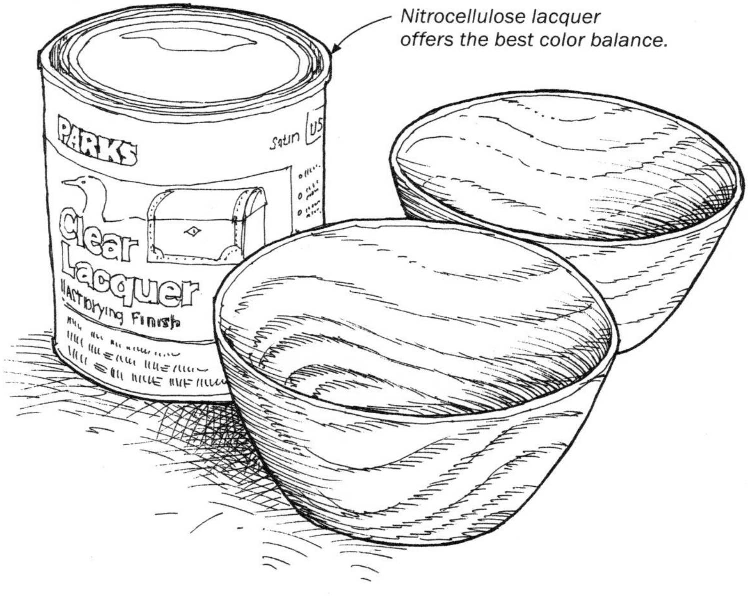
Nitrocellulose lacquer
offers the best color balance.
PARKS
Satin
Clear
Lacquer
Finish

HERE'S MY ADVICE TO WOODWORKERS searching for a colorless finish that does not impart any color to the underlying wood in wooden bowls: Stop searching—it does not exist. But take heart, some finishes come pretty close. Each resin in a finishing system contributes a characteristic color to the final product. Acrylic resins impart a slightly bluish tint that is especially visible on light-colored woods such as maple and holly. Heavy acrylic coatings give the finished piece a cold, plastic look that I find objectionable. Oil-based varnishes are distinctly yellow. These finishes obscure the subtle color highlights common in cabinet hardwoods. Varnishes also dramatically change the color of many exotic woods, like padauk and purpleheart.

In my opinion, nitrocellulose lacquers offer the best color balance among all the common woodworking finishes. These light amber-colored finishes add warmth and depth to the wood. And nitrocellulose lacquers accentuate the color and the figure of the wood rather than hide it like varnish finishes tend to do.

—CHRIS MINICK, *Stillwater, Minn.,*
from a question by Peter H. Rohr, Hilton Head Island, S.C.

Watco-Deft Finish

MY CHOICE FOR A DINING-ROOM table finish that's both durable and attractive combines a prime coat of Watco Danish oil with following coats of Deft lacquer. Here's the method: Brush on a sloshing coat of Watco over the prepared surface, let it soak in, and then wipe it thoroughly with a clean, absorbent lint-free cloth. Let it sit for at least 24 hours, and then rub it down with 0000 steel wool, taking care to rub in the direction of the grain. Allow it to sit for another two to three days, depending on the humidity, until the Watco has gotten fairly hard and won't interfere with the adhesion of the Deft to come.

Now spray or brush on a thick, wet coat of Deft lacquer, as much as the surface will take without developing runs. When this coat is completely dry, sand it in the direction of the grain with 220-grit paper, using a padded block. Spray on another full coat, and when it is dry, sand with 400-grit paper. Repeat this step. The fourth coat is also a full-strength application, but it should be steel-wooled, not sanded.

—Morris Sheppard,
from a question by John Millerd, Pemberton Meadows, B.C., Canada

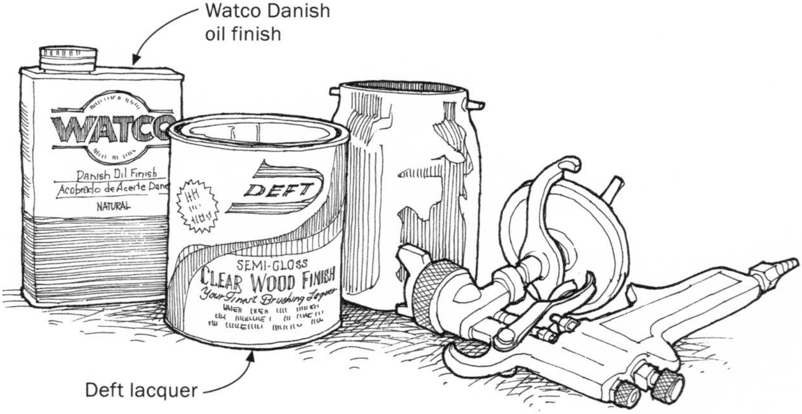

Painting Polyurethaned Kitchen Cabinets

I was recently asked to recommend a white-pigmented surface coating to cover dark-stained and polyurethane-varnished cabinets. One option for coating the cabinets would be a two-part epoxy paint such as Imron catalyzed finish or Sherwin-Williams' Polane. These products would be excellent choices for refurbishing or upgrading your existing kitchen cabinets. The finish produced by any one of these systems will far surpass the National Kitchen and Bath Association (NKBA) standards for food-stain resistance and durability. But, unless you are very familiar and comfortable with spray application of reactive finishing materials, I would avoid these finishing systems. It takes a lot of patience and practice with these finishes to achieve acceptable results. But fortunately, an acceptable refurbishing alternative does exist.

Ideally, any restoration project should include removal of the old finish, as this gives you the widest choice of subsequent finishes. Finishing over the existing polyurethane varnish on your kitchen cabinets narrows your choices to either pigmented oil-based alkyd or uralkyd products. These are materials that bond satisfactorily to cured polyurethane varnish. To simulate the modern high-gloss plastic-laminate look, follow the steps below. If you would like the existing grain patterns to show in the final finish, omit the grain-filling step.

First, remove the cabinet doors (and face frames if possible). Thoroughly wipe all surfaces with lacquer thinner to remove any condensed cooking oils or other contaminants. Now scuff-sand the existing finish with 180-grit sandpaper and apply a quality grain filler to the doors and face frames. Paste grain fillers, especially the oil-based type, take a very long time to dry, so allow at least two days drying time before proceeding. Sand the dried doors and face frames with progressively finer sandpaper to 220 grit. Wipe the surface with a tack cloth to remove any remaining sanding dust. Finally, brush apply two or three coats of a high-gloss, slow-drying alkyd enamel. Brand names are unimportant, but I personally think that Sherwin-Williams' All Surface Enamel would work best in your situation. Regardless of the brand used, allow several days for it to cure before reinstalling doors and face frames. Although this finishing system would not pass the NKBA durability tests, it offers adequate protection for everyday use. If the finish does become damaged, recoating is an easy task.

—Chris Minick, *Stillwater, Minn.,*
from a question by W.J. Zahorchak, Roanoke, Va.

Water-Repellent Exterior Finish

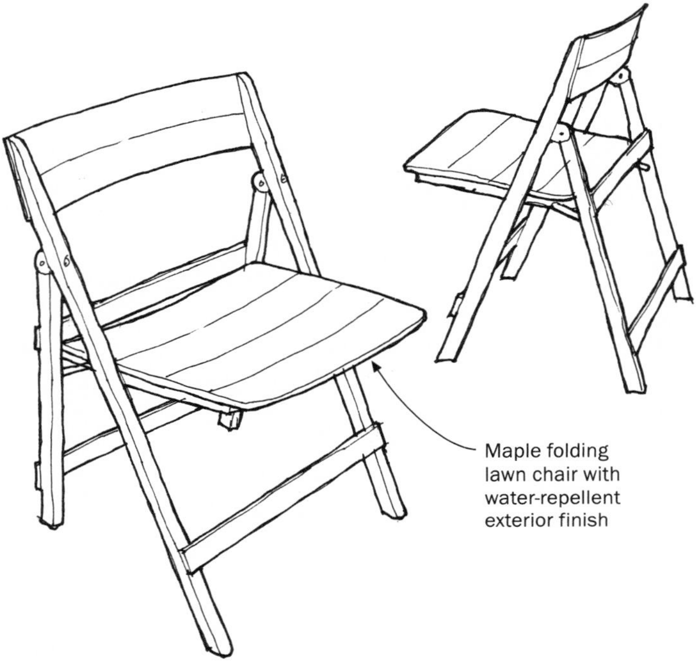

HERE'S A FINISH FORMULA I'D RECOMMEND for old-fashioned maple folding chairs or any outdoor furniture. It will withstand summer wear and resist water and humidity. Start with a good indoor/outdoor phenolic resin-based spar varnish. Masury paint makes an excellent product called Cosmo Spar (available from local hardware and paint supply dealers) that dries in four hours. After sanding the chair with 220-grit paper and wiping off the dust with a tack cloth, thin the varnish 50/50 with mineral spirits and apply with a brush or cloth. Let it dry overnight. Sand smooth with 220-grit paper and wipe again with the tack cloth, then apply a second coat of the 50/50 solution. For the third coat, apply a mixture of three-parts varnish to one-part mineral spirits. Let the third coat dry overnight, then sand with 320-grit paper. The fourth and final coat is full-strength varnish. When the last coat has dried, you many want to dull the gloss with 000 steel wool and polish the surface with a good grade of wax. This finish is very durable and resistant to summer humidity.

—BEAU BELAJONAS, *Camden, Maine, from a question by Berton LeBlanc, Moncton, N.B., Canada*

Achieving a Flat Surface with Polyurethane Varnish

POLYURETHANE IS A DURABLE interior finish, but it's nearly impossible to get a clean, flat surface when it's applied full strength for three or more coats. One trick I've found is to start with spar varnish thinned 50/50 with turpentine. Apply this first coat with a clean, lint-free cotton cloth shaped like a French-polishing rubber. The second coat is thicker (75/25) and is applied with a bristle brush, followed upon drying by light sanding to remove dust and flecks. Then apply a third coat (gloss or satin) full strength with a foam-rubber brush. If any surface irregularities appear, they can be smoothed out with a light touch from a cabinet scraper. Then I rub with 000 steel wool, followed by vigorous rubbing with a cotton cloth. Finally, I apply Trewax with 000 steel wool, buffing it just prior to drying. A second coat of wax will give a higher luster, but this time it should dry completely before it's buffed.

—RICHARD C. OLLIG, *Maryville, Tenn.*

Finishes for Outdoor Furniture in the Humid Gulf Coast

FINDING THE RIGHT FINISHES FOR OUTDOOR furniture in the humid gulf coast is difficult, even for furniture made from durable and rot-resistant woods like cypress. The two big culprits are mildew and deterioration due to UV rays in sunlight. In the right conditions, mildew will form on any finished surface, and mildew may even feed on oil. Nevertheless, your best option for a clear exterior finish is a tung-oil and phenolic-resin varnish. The ultraviolet (UV) rays present in sunlight will adversely affect most clear finishes, but a good exterior varnish containing UV "blockers" will resist this degradation considerably longer, though not indefinitely. When the finish does start to deteriorate, if you catch it before it peels or cracks, you can sand it lightly and recoat with more varnish without having to strip the finish entirely.

A widely available tung oil/phenolic varnish is McCloskey's Man-'O-War. Although this does not contain added UV blockers, the phenolic resin contains some natural sun blockers. Although more expensive, McCloskey's Boat Koat is a pure tung oil/phenolic mix with added UV blockers, and it is great for outdoor use. Not all dealers stock Boat Koat, though; if you have trouble finding it, call McCloskey's (now owned by Val Spar) at (800) 323-5129 for your nearest dealer.

—MICHAEL DRESDNER, *Zionhill, Pa., from a question by Marland Mendoza, Gonzales, La.*

Choosing a Long-Lasting Boat Finish

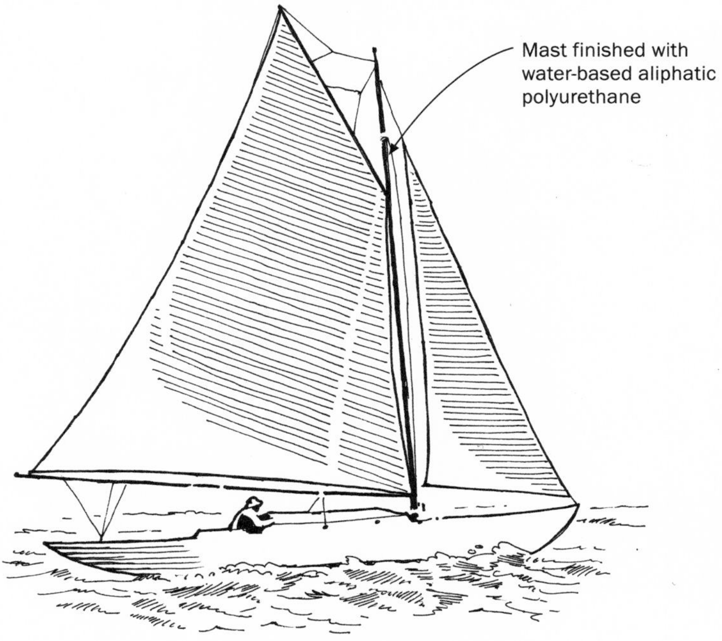

A FRIEND RECENTLY PURCHASED A SAILBOAT with a 28-ft.-long mast made of Sitka spruce and asked me about the best way to finish it. He had consulted with the previous owner, who removed the mast and refinished it every one to two years with a clear spar varnish.

I explained that spar varnish originally gained popularity among boatbuilders because its high degree of flexibility allowed it to last through the drastic changes in humidity a boat encounters. However, spar varnish is hardly the most durable of finishes. Recently, molecular architects have developed new and better polymers that combine durability with flexibility and throw in many favorable exterior properties as well.

My choice for longevity would be a water-based aliphatic polyurethane, such as Hydrocote Polyshield (available from Highland Hardware, 1045 N. Highland Ave. N.E., Atlanta, GA 30306; 404-872-4466). Aromatic urethanes are not ultraviolet (UV) light stable and thus should be avoided. For that matter, any product chosen should have UV absorbers as well as hindered amine light stabilizers (HALS) for the optimum life expectancy. In use, these finishes should last at least three times as long as spar varnish.

—MICHAEL DRESDNER, *Perkasie, Pa.,*
from a question by David P. Biddle, Natural Bridge Station, Va.

Finish for Cedar Siding

WHEN YOU'RE CONSIDERING EXTERIOR paints and stains for cedar siding use this general rule: The more pigment a finish has, the longer it will last.

Paint is the best protection. Three coats (one primer and two top coats) are needed for protection that will last six to ten years on smooth wood.

Semitransparent oil-based stains are the next most durable finish. These contain some pigment. On new, smooth cedar, they'll last two to four years; rough or weathered cedar will be protected for three to six years.

A water-repellent preservative is a relatively simple natural finish. These products are easy to apply and reapply, but will last only one to two years on new, smooth wood, and two to four years on rough or weathered wood.

—WILLIAM FEIST, *Madison, Wisc.,*
from a question by Albert Feers, Newbury Park, Calif.

Finish for a Windsor Chair

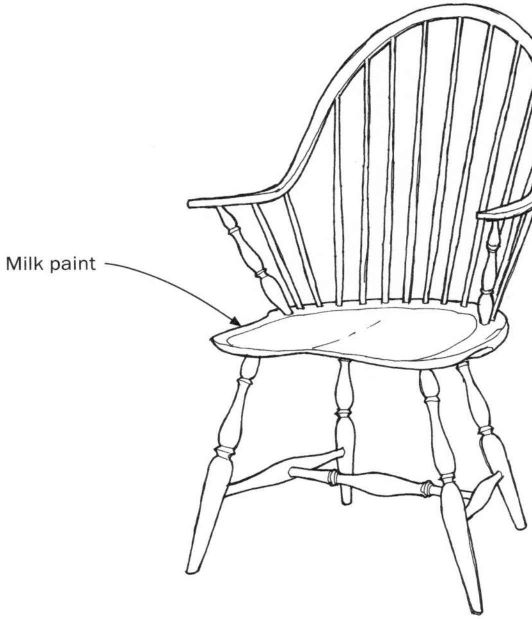

TO SET THE BACKGROUND FOR WINDSOR CHAIR finishes, let's go back to the Federal period (1780-1810), when most American Windsor styles were developed. Then Windsor chairs were always painted—green being the most popular color. It's often said that Windsors were painted only to cover the different woods that make up the chair but I disagree. Instead, I believe that the painted surface existed in the chairmaker's mind before the chair design did and that Windsors look the way they do because of this choice of finish. If the wood was meant to be seen, Windsor designs would be very different.

A lot of utilitarian furniture in the Windsor era was painted. Wood was perceived simply as an abundant, versatile material. Today, however, when so much of our furniture is made of chrome and plastic, our perception of wood is different. For us, wood is precious—a link to the natural world. The phrase "natural beauty of wood" has become a cliché and a clear finish has become an extension of that cliché. Painted furniture goes against current fashion.

To use a natural finish on a Windsor, however, is to try to separate the chair from the paint around which it was designed. Color coalesces the verticals, horizontals, and curves of a Windsor into a whole and prevents the eye from being distracted as it moves along the lines of the chair. The different woods in a Windsor were selected not for what they looked like but for the physical characteristics of the species. When these woods are visible, the different colors of the oak, birch, and pine are distracting. As a result, one tries to turn the chair into a uniform shade of brown with chemicals and stains. In other words, one tries to paint with dyes instead of paint.

I finish my Windsors with milk paint because it resembles the original lead-based painted finish (available from The Old-Fashioned Milk Paint Co., Box 222, Groton, MA 01450).

—MICHAEL DUNBAR, *Portsmouth, N.H.*

Finishing a Redwood Picnic Table

HERE'S HOW I WOULD FINISH a redwood picnic table. First, redwood is so beautiful it doesn't need any stain to enhance it. It also resists fungus and weather quite well. Mix equal amounts of boiled linseed oil and any good brand of varnish. Spread this mixture generously on the furniture, but before it dries—about 15 minutes to a half-hour later—wipe off all that you possibly can. Use a burlap-type rag, and plenty of elbow grease. The very thin coating that remains in the wood will offer surprisingly good protection and it can be improved by applying more coats. Give each application a week to dry and put the emphasis on the rubbing—that is what makes it beautiful.

—GEORGE FRANK,
from a question by Jonathan Wagman, Ulster Park, N.Y.

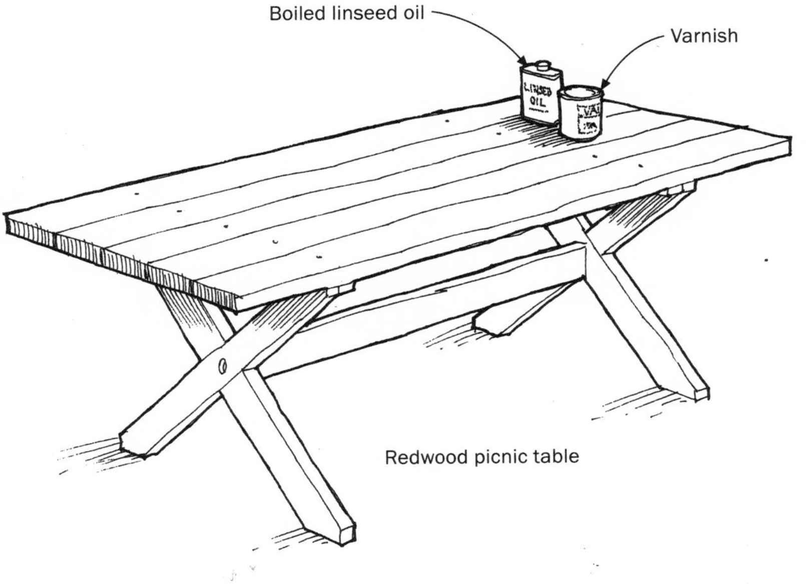

Restoring an Oak Relic

A FRIEND IS RESTORING A CIVIL WAR CANNON with a carriage made of native burr oak. When completed, the cannon will be constantly exposed to weather, and the wood will be painted. After some research with the U.S. Forest Products Laboratory in Madison, Wisc., we decided to use this three-step procedure to achieve a durable, exterior paint job: treatment with a water-repellent preservative, followed by priming, and finally two coats of a high-quality exterior paint. Water-repellent preservatives containing pentachlorophenol (such as Penta) are no longer available, but any preservative that contains copper naphtenate or copper-8-quinolinolate will function equally well. The Cuprinol line of water-repellent preservatives, manufactured by Darworth, Inc. (Box K, Tower Lane, Avon, CT 06001), contain the mentioned chemicals. These products are available at most hardware stores and home centers. Soaking the wood in preservative is by far the best method for treatment; allow the preservative to dry for several days before proceeding with the finishing sequence.

Two coats of exterior-grade primer should be applied next. Tests conducted by the U.S. Forest Products Laboratory indicate that a pigmented-shellac primer provides excellent protection against moisture vapor transmission, the enemy of all exterior-paint jobs. BIN White Pigmented Shellac Primer Sealer (made by William Zinsser & Co., 39 Belmont Drive, Somerset, NJ 08873) would be a good choice for your project.

Finally, apply two coats of exterior paint. It matters little if the paint is oil base or water base; equivalent results can be expected with either coating. My personal preference would be a 100% acrylic latex paint.

The acrylic systems provide excellent protection from the elements and resist yellowing better than most oil-base systems. It's worth mentioning that a wealth of wood finishing information can be obtained by writing to the U.S. Department of Agriculture Forest Service, Forest Products Laboratory, Madison, WI 53705. Ask for the wood-finishing list of publications. Most pamphlets are free or available for a minimal cost.

—Chris Minick, *Stillwater, Minn.,*
from a question by H. Richard Fishbaugh, Shenandoah, Iowa

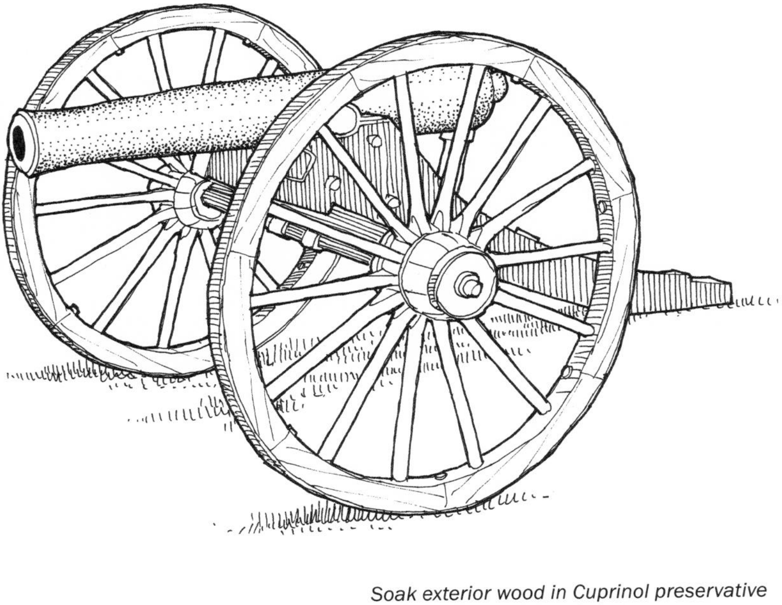

Soak exterior wood in Cuprinol preservative before priming and painting.

SHELLAC
FLAKES
S-L-X
Denatured
Alcohol

Chapter 2

NONTOXIC FINISHES

Nontoxic Toy Finishes

Behlen Salad Bowl Finish is nontoxic for children's toys.
BEHLEN
Salad Bowl Finish
CLEAR

SMALL CHILDREN PUT EVERYTHING in their mouths—including wooden toys. And there's a real concern that many paints, varnishes and oil finishes might contain chemicals that are harmful when ingested. In searching for safe finishes the first, and safest, finish to consider is, of course, no finish at all. But if you want to use one, the safest choice is a finish that's labeled "nontoxic." Behlen's Salad Bowl Finish (available from Garrett Wade, 161 Avenue of the Americas, New York, NY 10013) is a clear sealer that contains only ingredients approved by the Food and Drug Administration (FDA) for use in contact with food. Orr-Lac spray enamel (made by Spray Products Corp., P.O. Box 737, Norristown, PA 19404) is nontoxic when dry. Clear nitrocellulose lacquer, shellac, mineral oil, vegetable oil, and beeswax are also acceptable finishes.

To determine if other commercial finishes are safe for toys, read the label. If the product contains a metal such as lead, zinc, chromium, cobalt, antimony, selenium, barium, arsenic, mercury, or cadmium, it isn't safe to chew. Many commercial oil finishes—even tung oil or boiled linseed oil—fall into this category because they often contain toxic metal driers. All exterior finishes should be considered unsafe because most have mercury compounds to inhibit mildew. Paints and primers sold for use on metal often contain poisonous zinc chromate as a rust inhibitor. Pigments such as titanium dioxide, iron oxide, and carbon black and ingredients such as silica and silicates are often present in black, white, or earth-tone paints. They're harmless if ingested in small amounts.

Even if a finish passes the label test, you might also write to the manufacturer. Ask for a product-safety sheet, and ask if its finish is safe to use on infants' toys—just to be sure.

—GEORGE MUSTOE, *Bellingham, Wash.,*
from a question by Emma Wynn, Stroudsburg, Pa.

Toxicity Problems with Tung Oil

TUNG OIL IS OFTEN RECOMMENDED for salad bowls and children's toys. While tung oil itself is safe, the possibility exists that any particular brand of tung oil many contain some metallic driers. The reason I do not recommend tung oil for the above application is because I think it is best to be absolutely sure you have a lead-free or mercury-free finish wherever there is a possibility of its being ingested. The bottom line is that tung oil, unless specifically labeled as nontoxic, is not suitable for surfaces that may come in contact with food or for children's toys.

—DON NEWELL, *Farmington, Mich.,*
from a question by Michael McGrath, East Dubuque, Ill.

Child-Safe Finishes for Jigsaw Puzzles

RECENTLY I WAS ASKED if the spray fixatives, like those found in art supply stores, are safe finishes for children's jigsaw puzzles. The concern was that the fixatives contain acetone and toluene, solvents that are sufficiently hazardous to be singled out on warning labels on the can.

First, let me say that the hazard warnings printed on the label pertain to the material in the can, not necessarily to the toxicity of the dried finish. Adequate ventilation, proper protective equipment, and some common sense will protect you from the adverse effects of most finishes during application.

Most finishes are totally safe once the solvents have evaporated. However, when making projects for small children, it's still wise to select a finish known to be safe. Two child-safe finishes immediately come to mind: shellac and walnut oil.

Shellac, the processed excretion of a tiny insect, has been used for hundreds of years as a lacquer-like furniture finish and is the main ingredient of a traditional French polish.

The nontoxic nature of dried shellac is well documented. In fact, shellac is approved by the FDA as an additive for foods and pharmaceuticals. Shellac is used to make glazes found on some cookies and candy, as well as the timed-release coating found on some pills.

I prefer to mix my own shellac (dry shellac flakes dissolved in denatured alcohol), but the premixed, hardware-store variety also will work. Shellac has a short shelf life once mixed; old shellac doesn't dry well. If you use the premixed variety, test to see how long it takes to dry on scrap. After half an hour, it should no longer feel tacky.

Pure walnut oil, a semidrying oil pressed from walnut meats, is my finish of choice for wooden cooking utensils and cutting boards. Walnut oil dries slowly (usually in about five days) and forms a soft, easily damaged film. It's probably not ideal for jigsaw puzzles, but it does make a good finish for toys.

Walnut oil can be applied just like any other finishing oil. Apply a heavy coat, let it soak for 30 minutes, and then wipe off the excess. When the toys begin to look a little battered from use, just apply another coat to rejuvenate the finish.

I would avoid water-based finishes or floor waxes on wooden puzzles. The water in either of these will raise the grain, and sanding all those puzzle pieces would be a lot of work.

—CHRIS MINICK, *Stillwater, Minn.,*
from a question by Del Fussell, Englewood, Colo.

Nontoxic Paraffin Finish

PARAFFIN WAX MAKES A GOOD nontoxic finish for wooden toys, butcher blocks, and countertops. Warm the wood, then rub on paraffin that's been melted in a double boiler (melt it carefully—paraffin is extremely flammable). The finish is safe, nonstaining, and can be polished to a dull luster.

—KEITH HACKER, *Scandia, Minn.*

Finishing Children's Toy Blocks

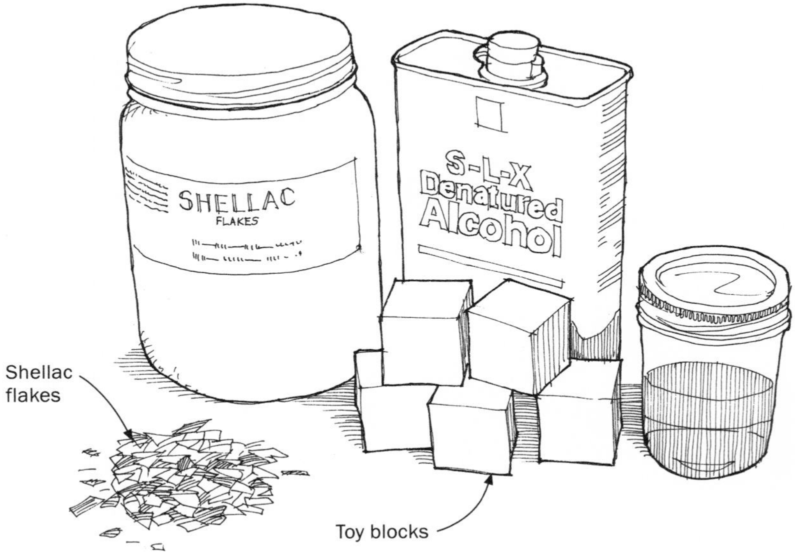

WHEN WOOD SCRAPS START overflowing the scrap bin, many of us are tempted to cut them into toy blocks for our children or grandchildren. But many woods, contain some compounds that could adversely affect health if consumed in a high enough dose. These compounds, however, pose very little risk when put in the mouth for a short while, so I doubt that blocks of any of the common species such as oak, poplar, cherry, and ash would be harmful to a child.

The bigger risk is asphyxiation. Children, especially toddlers, have an irresistible urge to put everything in their mouths. It's critically important the blocks be large enough to prevent a child from getting one stuck in his throat.

Oak contains high levels of tannic acid, and pine contains resins and terpenes. If a child were to gnaw on either of these woods vigorously, the result could be a very memorable bellyache.

Cherry produces cyanide-like compounds, which are potentially lethal, but they tend to concentrate in the fruit and foliage of the tree. The wood is not known for causing fatalities.

Walnut contains a substance called juglone, which is both a sedative and a laxative. I never use walnut when I'm making toys or kitchen utensils, though I'm probably being overly cautious.

Still, using a finish is a good idea. Blocks will stay bright and clean. Also, a finish will seal the grain, making it less likely the child will pick up any splinters or that germs will establish a home in the pores of the wood. But be sure to select a finish that you know to be nontoxic. Shellac is probably your best bet.

—JON ARNO, *Troy, Mich.,*
from a question by Edward G. Trzeciak, Ligonier, Pa.

Nontoxic Finishes from Plant Oils

IF YOU ARE LOOKING TO APPLY a nontoxic finish, you can also use coconut oil or lemon oil, neither of which will decay. Of course, any oil finish will be far better if it is applied hot and rubbed with 600-grit paper soaked with the oil of choice.

—MARTY SWEET, *Fairfax, Calif.*

Finish for Wooden Snack Bowls

ZAR polyurethane is certified nontoxic by the manufacturer.

As a finish for wooden bowls for snacks, like pretzels, you need a finish that is nontoxic, impermeable to oils, tough, and quick drying. This combination of characteristics is hard to find. For snack bowls I would try either a standard polyurethane or a moisture-cured urethane. These finishes have nearly all the characteristics you're looking for. No manufacturer I've contacted will recommend its finish for use with food or toys because of liability problems—this is understandable.

The question of toxicity arises mostly where a finish is exposed to liquids long enough or often enough to leach metallic compounds out of the finish and into the food. For only occasional use, even with liquid food, I would anticipate no problems with polyurethanes. They are very chemical resistant once they are thoroughly dry. Watco Danish Oil might also serve your purpose, as long as you let it cure for about 30 days to complete polymerization.

—DON NEWELL, *Farmington, Mich.,*
from a question by Thomas A. Laser, Springfield, Va.

THANK YOU FOR THE RECENT advice on finishes for bowls. Shortly after writing you, I wrote to United Gilsonite Laboratories in Scranton, Pa., the makers of ZAR polyurethanes. I was happy to hear that ZAR is nontoxic and suitable for bowls and other food utensils.

—THOMAS A. LASER, *Springfield, Va.*

Kitchen Countertop Finish

FOR FINISHING A WOOD KITCHEN countertop, how about using moisture-curing urethane such as is used on bar tops/bowling alleys/gymnasium floors? The wood must first be sealed properly with a compatible lacquer sealant. Check out the products of Hughson Chemical Company, Erie, PA 16512. They're tough but flexible, and the glasslike surface does not mar easily. It will be alcohol resistant, too.

—C. HABER, *Huntington Beach, Calif.*

Beeswax and Olive Oil Finish for Wooden Spoons

HERE'S HOW I FINISH GREEN wooden spoons with beeswax and olive oil. When carving spoons from green wood, you can tell with experience when the piece is about to check. Work in the shade, and take chances with only the poorest pieces. Carve the least stable woods outdoors on rainy days. Just before you think a piece is going to check, bury it in a pile of wet leaves or shavings or snow or under a wet towel. When the going really gets rough (lilac cut six months ago will check in about five minutes once you start working it), I keep the whole batch in a tub of water, carving a minute or two in each piece and tossing it back into the water until I wind up with a tub full of spoons.

Then I oil the rough-carved pieces as often as it takes until they won't take anymore. When they've shown a gloss for a week or two they are probably ready to fire.

For the third step, I fire in a mixture of beeswax and olive oil. I have never weighed or measured anything. I just melt the wax and add the oil until the cooled mixture can be softened by friction between the bare hands and the wood. The harder the mixture the better it is, as long as you are able to work it cold.

The spoons are immersed in this mixture at the minimum temperature required to vaporize the remaining moisture in the wood. You will see the surface of the liquid foam and roil. This process tires the mixture and, therefore, more wax must be added with every firing to keep it sufficiently hard. When it appears that all the moisture has been boiled out of the wood, I allow the oven to cool and remove the spoons from the wax/oil mixture just about as soon as I can with my bare hand.

Next, I lay the fired spoons outdoors for a week or two and allow the sun to draw out some of the oil (leaving, it seems, more wax behind). The longer you wait, the easier the spoons are to finish. As a last step, I finish by scraping and sanding, scrubbing well with soap and water and hanging each to dry before each sanding. Finally, I rub in some of the wax/oil mixture and polish with a cloth.

—DAN DUSTIN,
from a question by William C. Pellouchoud, Boulder, Colo.

Nontoxic Finishes

IF YOU ARE BUILDING CHILDREN'S wooden toys and want only to use finishes that are suitable for children to chew or lick, beware: There is no legal definition of "nontoxic," even though the phrase appears on many children's products. Toxicity is a relative term, and as the old grizzlies say, "Even water's toxic if you keep your head under long enough." The concern with finishing children's wooden toys is metallic driers (lead or mercury, for example) in the finishing material. When I finish toys for the kids in our family, I avoid any film formers that have driers listed on the label. A thin film of air-drying lacquers (water or solvent), shellac, and wax are possibilities.

Lacquer is fine, but if the wood is an oily species like teak or pine, a thin coat of brushed-on shellac will adhere better. Once dry, rub the finish smooth with some steel wool, and polish with paste wax. Shellac is also used as a candy coating to keep food coloring off your hands, so it's a good choice.

Another finish I use on toys is soybean oil from the grocer. It's a semidrying oil that is wiped on with a paper towel and ready to use in a few hours. It doesn't build up a film like shellac or lacquer, so it may not give the wet look some people desire. But it's easy to reapply. I use it on my maple and mahogany bowls, walnut and teak cutting boards, and walnut toys. Unlike animal fats, vegetable oils will not become rancid, so there's no worry about a foul smell over time.

—NANCY LINDQUIST, *Chicago, Ill.,*
from a question by Marvin Esser, Willowdale, Ont., Canada

Finishing a Salad Bowl

THERE ARE SEVERAL GOOD BOWL finishes on the market. Clear epoxy varnish applied in successive coats (see *Fine Woodworking* #23, May '80, p. 60) makes a hard and durable finish and it will not react with food or drink or dissolve in vinegar. Some craftsmen use plain mineral oil, though this finish requires a periodic reapplication of oil. My favorite treatment for bowls is Behlen Salad Bowl Finish (available from Woodcraft Supply, 313 Montvale Ave., Woburn, MA 01888). I prefer to rub in a couple of thin coats to seal the wood, though you can use the stuff more liberally if you want a built-up finish. I burnish the bowl to a soft luster. Light recoating is required from time to time, depending on the thickness of the original film.

—R. BRUCE HOADLEY, *Amherst, Mass., from a question by Ray J. Gormly, Prior Lake, Minn.*

Alcohol-Proof Sealer for Wine Goblets

THE BEST FINISH I'VE FOUND for wine goblets and other utensils is No. 100 clear gloss epoxy from the Peterson Chemical Corp. (704 S. River St., Sheboygan, WI 53081). The ingredients in the finish are approved by the FDA for use on utensils. The only restriction I've found in nine years of using the finish is that you can't wash it in a dishwasher, although warm soapy water is okay. For best results, make sure your goblets are dry before applying the finish, or the epoxy will bubble and discolor. When I turn green wood, for example, I store the bowls for several weeks in a room with 30% to 40% humidity, then bake them in a 150°F oven for five to seven hours. For maximum penetration, I thin the first coat 10% to 20% with No. 711 epoxy thinner. I apply five or six more full-strength coats, sanding lightly with 180-grit white silicon-carbide paper between coats. The epoxy seems to go on most easily and harden best when it's applied in a relatively warm 80°F room. For a natural satin finish, I sand the last coat lightly with 320-grit silicon-carbide paper. Finally, I buff the finish by hand with 00, 000, and 0000 steel wool. Make sure you apply the finish in a well-ventilated area.

—DAVID LORY, *Platteville, Wisc.,*
from a question by Alan Kaepplinger, Cary, Ill.

Nonallergenic Floor Finish

FOR A FLOOR FINISH THAT IS nonallergenic and contains no petroleum distillates, my first thought would be shellac. Shellac contains no petroleum distillates and makes a durable floor finish. Apply two thin coats, scuff-sanding between coats to remove whiskers. You'll get the maximum durability if the shellac penetrates the wood rather than builds up on top of it.

Tung oil is another possibility, although, in my view, it would not be as good as a floor finish. While it is extremely durable and resistant to liquids, it is probably not as wear-resistant. Also, pure tung oil dries flat—another reason I wouldn't choose it for finishing a floor.

—DON NEWELL, *Farmington, Mich.,*
from a question by Evan Fales, West Branch, Iowa

bondo

Chapter 3

SURFACE PREPARATION & REPAIR

Colored Wax Filler Pencils for Nail Holes

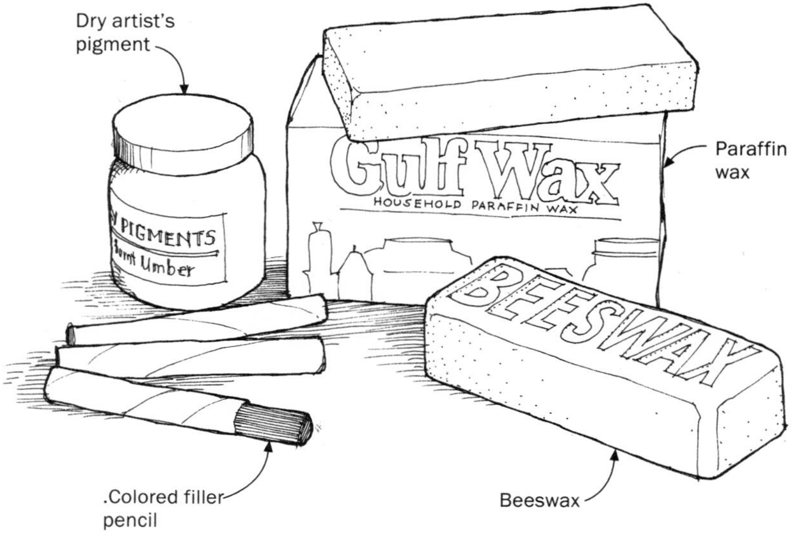

TO MAKE COLORED WAX FILLER PENCILS, melt equal quantities of beeswax and paraffin in a double boiler, add dry powdered pigments (available from art supply stores), then for every ounce of wax add a drop of linseed oil. You can make small paper tubes with one end closed and pour the well-stirred liquid into them. The oil will cause the wax to remain malleable. You can buy prepared burn-in sticks in a wide variety of colors, waxlike stain pencils, and dry pigments from Mohawk Finishing Products, Amsterdam, NY 12010.

—GEORGE FRANK, *South Venice, Fla., from a question by Jim Smith, Vancouver, B.C., Canada*

Wood-Dust Filler from Sanding Sealer

INSTEAD OF USING SAWDUST AND GLUE as a wood filler, use sawdust and sanding sealer. It dries quickly and will never leave a white spot, as the glue mixture will if not sanded off completely.

—MYRON MYKIWKA, *Guatemala City, Guatemala*

Wood Putty from Sanding Dust

THERE ARE SEVERAL WAYS TO MIX UP a low-cost wood putty from fine sanding dust, depending on the finish you plan to use. For a shellac or oil finish, mix the sanding dust with enough 2-lb.-cut shellac to give you the consistency of putty. If your piece is going to have a lacquer finish, mix the sanding dust with thinned lacquer. Both the shellac and lacquer putties can be stored in a sealed container, but I prefer to keep premixed liquid on hand and make the putty as I need it with dust from the piece I'm working on.

The shellac and lacquer filler won't take stain, so if you plan to stain your project, mix the sanding dust instead with either thin hot hide glue or yellow glue diluted 50% with water. Mix this as you need it because it won't keep for long.

Your homemade filler will be a little dark in the beginning but will eventually lighten. Apply enough filler so you can sand it flush after it dries.

—TAGE FRID,
from a question by Kenneth Copp, Philadelphia, Pa.

Making Dust for Wood-Dust Filler

AN EASY WAY TO GENERATE DUST to make wood filler is to turn a piece of wood on a lathe. With a gloved hand, hold a piece of sandpaper against the rotating piece. Sanding dust will quickly pile up on the sandpaper.

—BILL KADI, *Hayward, Calif.*

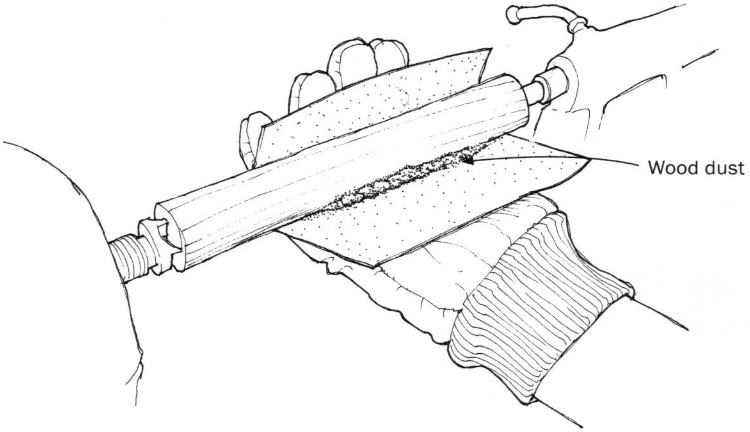

Stain before Filling the Pores or After?

WHEN FILLING THE PORES ON A WALNUT workpiece that you're going to stain and then oil, I think it's best to apply the stain before the filler. First, sand the wood with fine sandpaper, remove the dust, and wipe the surface clean. Then apply the stain with a rag and wipe off the excess. I prefer an oil-based, pigmented wiping stain somewhat lighter in color than the wood filler. You can use either walnut-colored filler or a natural paste wood filler colored to the desired shade with oil or oil-and-Japan colors, available from paint stores in small tubes. Reduce the filler following the instructions on the label, or mix equal volumes of paste filler and mineral spirits. Apply the filler with a brush, then follow up by padding the filler into the pores with a rag. When you see the solvent flash, scrub off the excess filler with a piece of burlap, wiping across the grain. You may need several coats to fill all of the large pores in the wood.

Finally, wipe with the grain using a clean cloth and very light strokes. Allow to dry in a warm room for 24 hours, then rub lightly with very fine steel wool. You may now apply a light coat of Watco or some other oil finish, but the oil won't penetrate the same as on unfilled wood. You may want to use only the oil wiping stain and omit the filler. If you do, let the stain dry for 24 hours and rub lightly with fine steel wool, then apply the final oil finish.

—OTTO H. HEUER, *Waukegan, Ill., from a question by Kenneth A. Sovereign, Aurora, Ill.*

Maintaining Luster with Oil Finishes

ON OCCASION THE DEPTH AND LUSTER that appears when you first flood the wood with an oil finish disappears when you wipe off the excess. When this happens, the problem is likely that your wood surface is not smooth enough. When you are dealing with oil finishes, remember that the finish is mainly in the wood, not on the surface. Oil has much less to do with the development of surface quality than other finishes—it just enhances what's already there. With oil finishes I suggest sanding the wood more with progressively finer grits, finishing up with a 220-, 280-, or even 320-grit before applying the oil.

—R. BRUCE HOADLEY, *Amherst, Mass., from a question by Mike Boehm, Madison, Wisc.*

Pre-Staining the Filler

WHEN I NEED TO FILL THE PORES in a stained piece, what I generally do is to sand the piece first and save the sawdust. I stain the dust with the same stain as is to be used on the piece and let the stained dust sit for a week or two. Then I stain the piece. After the stain has dried, I mix the stained dust with white glue and use it as a filler. After the filler has dried, I sand the piece in the filled areas and restain, and then put on whatever finish is desired. If the stain must or might be changed, I would hold off on staining the sawdust until the final stain color for the piece is selected. This approach takes advantage of the principle that no filler takes stain in the same manner as the wood in the piece.

—MICHAEL VOOLICH, *Somerville, Mass.*

Versatile Wood Filler

ONE OF THE BEST WOOD FILLERS I have discovered is Woodwise Full-Trowel Filler (manufactured by Design Hardwood Products, 16149 Redmond Way, Suite 118, Redmond, WA 98052; 206-869-0859). This product is a latex wood filler used on hardwood floors by flooring installers. Woodwise also works in other applications—tabletops, cabinets, etc., where it dries faster, shrinks less, and is easier to sand than putties sold for woodworking. The product is available in a number of common wood tones.

—CHRIS MINICK, *Stillwater, Minn.,*
from a question by Lawrence E. Daly, Barryton, Mich.

Making End Grain Look Great

TO EVEN OUT THE BLOTCHY EFFECT you often get in staining end grain, especially with open-grained woods like mahogany, your best bet is to size the end grain with hot hide glue before applying the finish. I have used this method with good results, and it does not change the color of the wood. You may have to experiment a little to get the knack of mixing the glue to the proper consistency. I mix the glue so that it drops from the brush like honey, then make a more dilute solution by mixing one part glue with two parts of hot water. Sand the end grain as smooth as you can, then brush the glue sizing on hot, say at about 180°F. After the sizing dries for about 24 hours, sand it with fine sandpaper and apply the finish.

—TAGE FRID,
from a question by Raymond Frances, Pelham, N.Y.

Repairing Knotholes with Auto-Body Filler

WHEN REPAIRING KNOTHOLES and other large defects, I use auto-body filler tinted to match the wood with dry pigments or oil colors. It sets up quickly and hard, doesn't shrink, and can be shaped with woodworking tools—Surforms work particularly well, especially before the filler has cured completely. Be sure to use a filler with red catalyst, not blue. The blue catalyst makes it more difficult to match the color of the wood.

—POPE A. LAWRENCE, *Santa Fe, N.M.*

Patching Holes with Acrylic Modeling Paste

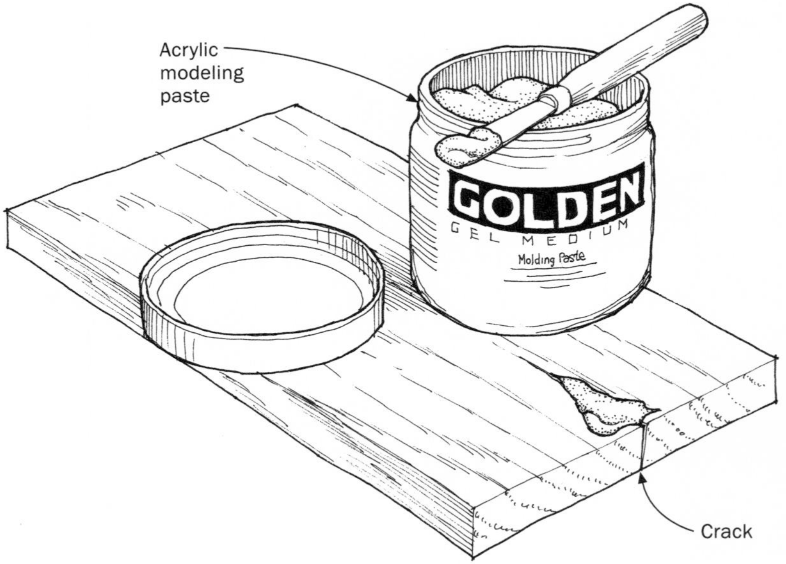

LIKE MANY OTHER CRAFTSMEN, I've been through the mill trying to find a suitable material for patching cracks, holes and other imperfections in wood projects. I finally hit upon a terrific solution: acrylic modeling paste—the kind artists use for thick, built-up effects. It's available at any well-stocked art supply shop. You can color the paste to match any wood, using commonly available acrylic artist's paints. The paste will go into hairline cracks and can be piled up about ⅛ in. thick without cracking. It carves, sands, and machines like wood. What's more, it will take any finish.

—JOHN STOCKARD, *Milledgeville, Ga.*

Patching Hairline Cracks with Cyanoacrylate Glue

HERE'S HOW TO REPAIR AND FILL a hairline crack that mars an otherwise usable piece of wood. You'll need fast-penetrating cyanoacrylate glue and extra-thick cyanoacrylate glue. Both are commonly available at hobby and model shops. If the crack is closed, hold it open with a knife. Apply the fast-penetrating glue first, which will be sucked deep into the crack by capillary action. Then apply the heavy-bodied glue, which will follow the thinner glue into the crack. Open and close the crack a few times to distribute the glue. If the crack is open, force wood dust into it with a spatula or an artist's palette knife and mix it with the glue. Clamp the wood if needed. Two hours is enough drying time.

—JOHN W. WOOD, *Tyler, Tex.*

Repairing Fancy Old Picture Frames

TO REPAIR AN OLD PICTURE FRAME with a missing section of decoration, I press modeling clay or warm paraffin over the existing decorative molding and allow it to cool in position. After cooling, it releases well and produces a very good mold that retains all the detail of the decoration. I then use a wood putty such as Durham Rock Hard, mix it into a stiff paste, and spread it into the clay mold using an artist's palette knife. Peel off the mold and you should have a perfect duplication of the missing part, which can be fitted and glued in place and finished to match.

—EDWIN T. HIRTE, *St. Paul, Minn., from a question by Charles Alger*

Raising Dents with a Clothes Iron

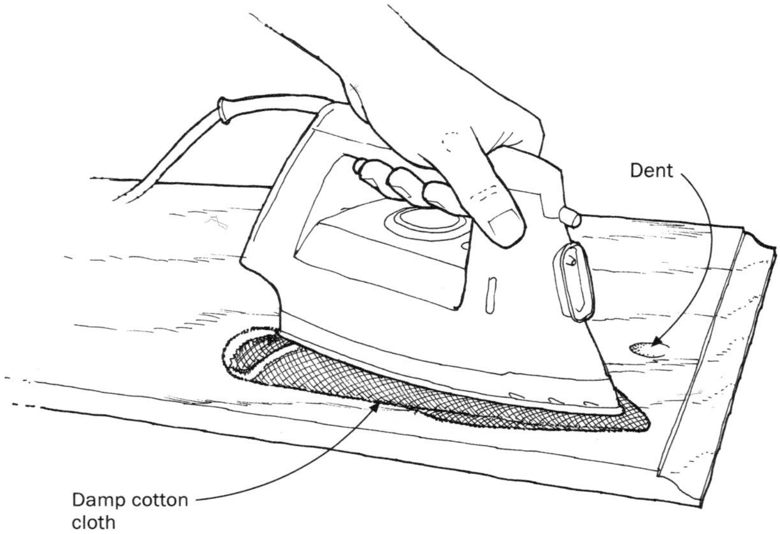

TO ELIMINATE OR REDUCE DENTS in wood, use a clothes iron or soldering iron, a natural-fiber, smooth-finish cloth folded to a point, water, and discretion.

Wet the dent, allowing the crushed fibers to soak up the water. Squeeze excess water out of the cloth. Bring the iron up to the boiling point but not to full heat. Test the wet cloth until it steams. Press the wet cloth into the dent with the hot iron for as long as steam is still produced. Repeat, if necessary, until no further rising occurs. You cannot burn the wood as long as the cloth is wet, so press the iron for brief intervals and be sure the cloth is continually wet. This should be done only on raw wood; if there is finish on the piece, remove the finish first.

Raise the dent before planing or scraping. Otherwise, the dent may rise above the planed surface. Make one or two passes with a plane at its finest setting after raising the dent.

This technique works as long as the dented fibers have been crushed and not torn.

—HENRY T. KRAMER, *Rye, N.Y.*

Keeping Your Coffee Warm

MY SHOP IRON STEAMS OUT A DENT only once in a while, but it does daily work keeping my coffee warm. The iron lives hot-side-up in a wall bracket that's bandsawn to hold it securely.

—ROBERT H. HOELZER, *Seattle, Wash.*

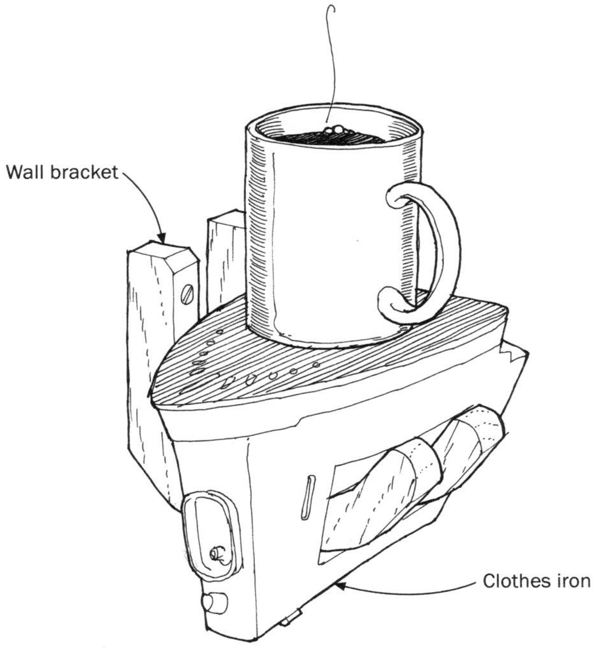

Clothes-Iron Shop Applications

AN ORDINARY CLOTHES IRON CAN simplify two furniture repairs: raising dents and reattaching loose veneer. To use the iron to remove dents and dings, set the heat to "cotton" or "wool," wet a cotton pad, and place it over the dent. Press the iron to the pad for two or three seconds and check your progress. Repeat the procedure until the dent is flush.

To repair loose veneer, place a damp cloth between the iron and the work. Apply the iron to the spot, taking care to move it about so as not to build up the heat too fast—the veneer will scorch if you're not careful. This method doesn't work with some adhesives, but most old furniture was veneered with hide glue, which will reactivate and hold the loose veneer down again.

—ROLLIE JOHNSON, *Sauk Rapids, Minn.*

Making Filler from Fine Sawdust

THERE ARE SEVERAL METHODS for making a hole-filling putty from fine sawdust taken right from the particular wood you are using. You can mix the sawdust with hide glue or with white cabinet glue. You can also mix it with liquid shellac, or you can mix it with clear lacquer.

—GEORGE FRANK, *South Venice, Fla.,*
from a question by G.C. Scates, Covina, Calif.

Low-Budget Composition Castings

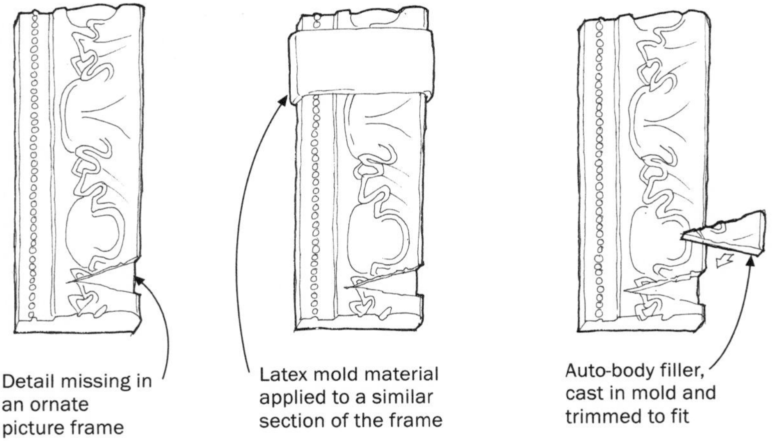

I RECENTLY RESTORED A 75-YEAR-OLD MIRROR FRAME that had much of the composition floral detail missing. Because of a tight budget, I had to find a low-cost way of duplicating the missing decoration. After several trials, I found a method that worked.

First make a mold of the existing decorative elements using latex mold material, commonly available at craft stores. Fill the mold with plastic auto-body filler. Just after the body filler starts to set up but is still in a plastic state, remove the cast from the mold. Trim the cast with a razor blade to make a piece that fits the missing section. The piece can be formed to fit a curved frame. Set the new piece in place, and weigh it down with a bag of sand until it is fully cured.

To ensure the cast does not stick to the frame prematurely, sprinkle talcum powder on the frame. After the cast has cured, you can easily cement it in place with a new batch of body filler. Then you're ready for finishing.

—SCOTT R. CARNEGIE, *Downers Grove, Ill.*

Repairing Missing Ornate Trim

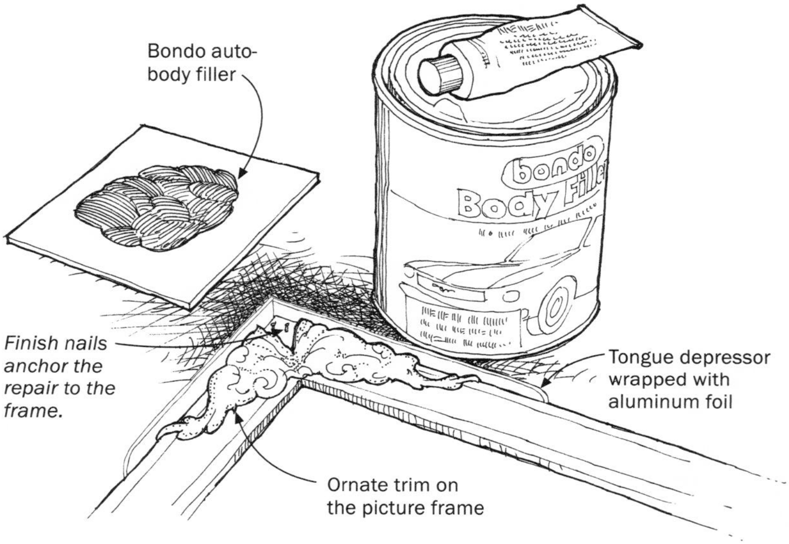

A PIECE OF FURNITURE MAY seem beyond repair if a large chunk of ornate trim is missing or damaged. The repairman may lack the skills to carve a new piece of wood, or the carving may cost more than the furniture itself. The answer is to make a mold from the existing trim and cast a new piece with auto body putty, better known as Bondo.

Bondo comes in two parts, a resin and a catalyst. It does not dry, but rather cures, and therefore (unlike plastic wood) does not shrink. When it has cured it can be shaped and drilled like wood. It won't absorb stain, but can be painted or colored with Blendal powdered stains (from Mohawk Chemical Co., Amsterdam, N.Y.) to match the surrounding wood.

To make a mold, remove a section of undamaged trim from the furniture and drive a couple of finishing nails into the back of it to act as handles. Fill a container with plaster of Paris, grease the front surface of the trim with any light oil, and push it firmly into the plaster. As you set the trim, wiggle it a bit to ensure a good contact and be careful not to let the plaster flow over the back of it. When the mold has hardened, use the nails to pull the trim out. The finish on it will be blushed by the moisture in the plaster, but it can be restored by using Mohawk's blender flow-out, which comes both glossy and flat.

You can now make new trim by greasing the mold and pouring Bondo into it. Stir gently to get rid of air bubbles. When the Bondo starts to cure, set a few nails in the back for handles so it can be pulled from the mold. After it is solid it can be pared with a knife, sanded, and cut to fill the damaged area on the furniture. Attach it with epoxy glue. Bondo continues to cure for about a week and if you wait too long to trim and sand it, it will be like steel.

Bondo can also be used to repair a damaged corner or other area where it isn't practical to make a mold from existing trim. First clean the damaged area and cut away any slivers of wood. Don't be afraid to enlarge it—another half-inch won't make any difference. Drive a few finishing nails into the damaged area to anchor the Bondo, but make sure the heads are below the undamaged surface. Now wrap aluminum foil around some small pieces of wood, such as tongue depressors, and tape them to the undamaged wood so they bridge the repair zone and act as a form for the Bondo. Trowel in the plastic, in layers if necessary, and when it cures remove the forms. You'll have a crude representation of the undamaged area, which can then be shaped with a knife and sandpaper.

—GLENN RATHKE, *Pompano Beach, Fla.*

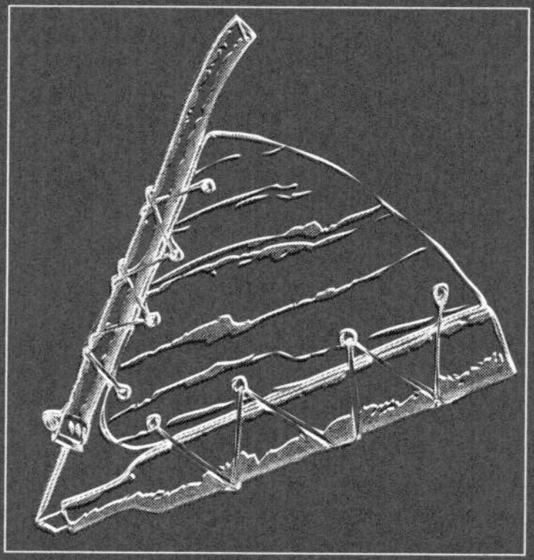

Chapter 4

TOOLS OF THE TRADE

Disposable Foam Brush

I USE THIS HOMEMADE FOAM BRUSH with its disposable insert on those little oil-finish or paint jobs where it would be more work to clean a brush than to do the job.

I fold ½-in.-thick foam carpet padding around the end of a $\frac{1}{32}$-in. aluminum stiffening strip, and clamp it with a rubber band in an aluminum holder. After the job is done, you can throw away the foam and wipe off the aluminum.

—HARRY M. MCCULLY, *Allegany, N.Y.*

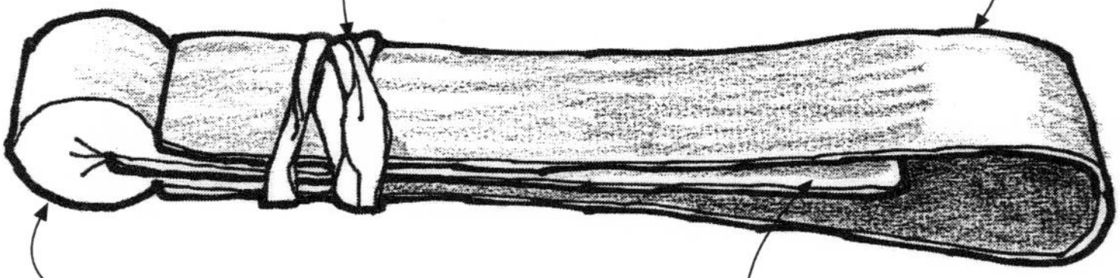

Finish Applicators from Upholstery Foam

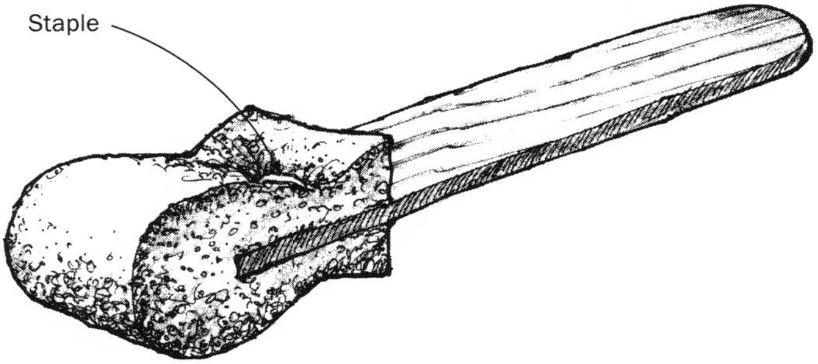

YOU CAN EASILY MAKE THROWAWAY FINISH applicators from urethane foam, which is commonly sold in fabric and upholstery shops. Cut the foam to a 1x1x2 size, split it down the middle and staple it to a scrap of thin wood for a handle. You can then trim the free end with scissors to suit the job.

—DAVID E. PRICE, *Baltimore, Md.*

USE CHUNKS OF HIGH-DENSITY FOAM, the kind made for upholstered furniture cushions, to quickly and evenly apply any type of oil finish. Buy 4-in.-thick pieces of foam and cut the applicators to the desired shape on your bandsaw.

—R. CHARLES BOELKINS, *Conyers, Ga.*

Disposable Swab

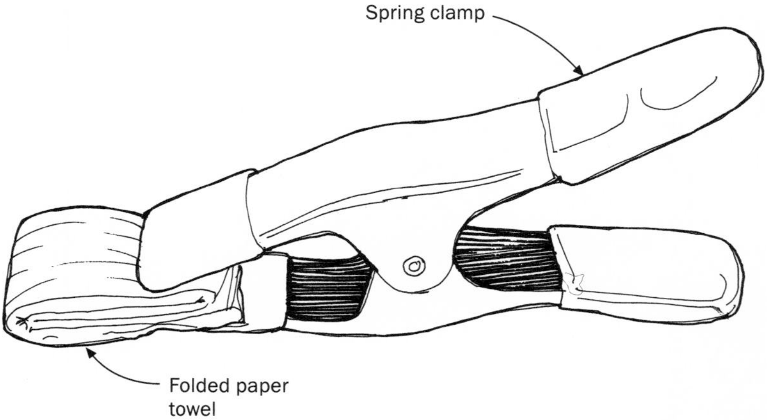

WHEN APPLYING A SMALL AMOUNT of stain or finish, I make a swab by tightly folding a piece of cloth or paper towel into a pad. I then lock the pad into a small vise-grip or a spring clamp, so I can hold it during use. When I'm finished applying the stain, I just throw away the pad.

—OMAR V. SHOWALTER, *Harrisonburg, Va.*

Graining Tool

TO MAKE A GRAINING TOOL THAT WORKS on any contour, including intricate molding, roll up a strip of inner tube and notch its end randomly on the bandsaw with cuts about ⅛ in. deep. Then using a glaze of artists' oil colors, linseed oil and varnish, you can produce a striking grain pattern—with practice.

—J. B. SMALL, *Newville, Pa.*

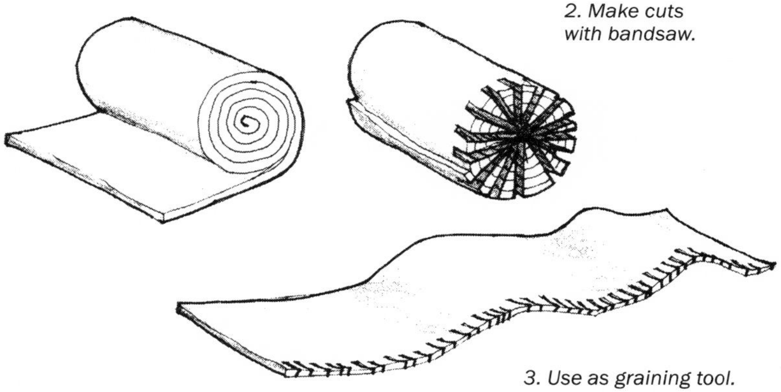
1. Roll up piece of inner tube.
2. Make cuts with bandsaw.
3. Use as graining tool.

Collapsible Finish Containers

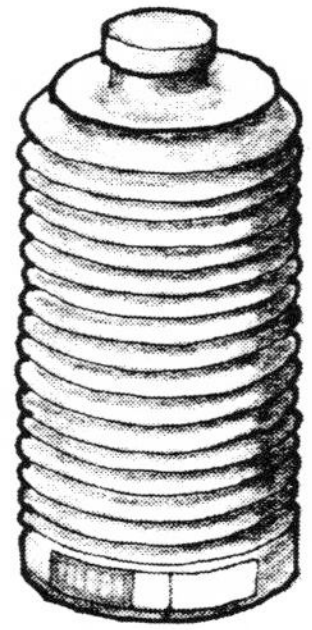

COLLAPSIBLE PLASTIC BOTTLES for photographic chemicals (available from photo supply houses) make excellent working and storage containers for tung oil and other finishing materials that skin over or polymerize in half-empty cans. As the finish is used up, the bottles can be folded like an accordion before the top is screwed on, which eliminates just about all of the air.

—T. CARPENTER, *Calgary, Alb., Canada*

Kitchen Baster Handy in Shop

TRANSFERRING LACQUER FROM a gallon can to your sprayer cup needn't be messy and awkward. Use a common kitchen baster like a jumbo eyedropper to transfer the finish. To maintain domestic tranquillity, don't steal the baster from your kitchen. Rather, go buy your own, making sure the body is nylon so that it is impervious to lacquer and lacquer thinner. The baster is useful in cleanup also. Use it to squirt solvent through spray gun orifices.

—CHUCK ANDERSON, *Porterville, Calif.*

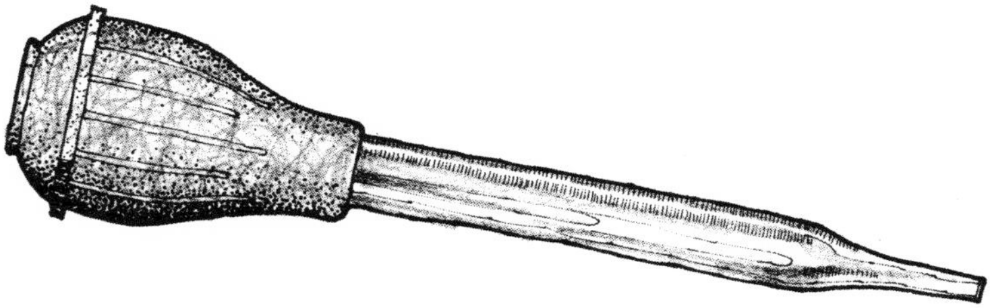

Low-Cost Airbrush

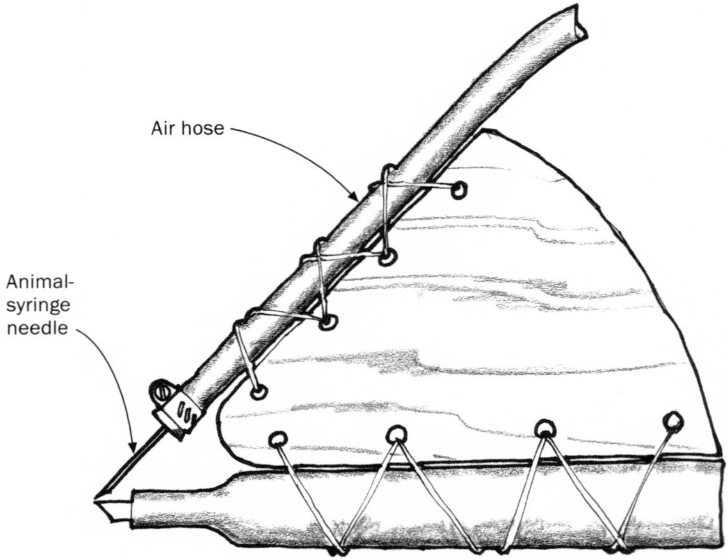

YOU CAN MAKE AN EFFECTIVE airbrush by using a needle from a No. 11 animal syringe and a common felt-tip marker. As shown in the sketch above, a simple wooden block with rubber bands holds the tip of the marker in the fine air stream that passes through the needle. For the air supply, use a shop compressor regulated at 15 to 30 psi. I recommend the use of an electric solenoid to start and stop the air with a minimum of bleed-off. I use the airbrush to detail fishing lures in a rainbow of colors.

—FRED J. STEFFENS, *Monroe, Wisc.*

Keeping a Paint-Can Lip Dry

WHEN I OPEN A CAN OF PAINT, I set the lid aside. In its place, I attach a previously used lid with a semicircular hole in it. The best shape for the opening is a half moon, with a straight edge near the middle and a curve following the outer edge of the rim—not too close, though. I stick my brush into the paint through the opening and use the flat edge to scrape excess paint from the brush. Or I pour the paint using the opening's corner. Through all this, the sealing lip of the can is protected from drips and remains clean. When I'm through, I just reattach the original lid. If the paint is used up, I save the lid for a future cutout.

—RONALD R. SCHULTZE, *Redlands, Calif.*

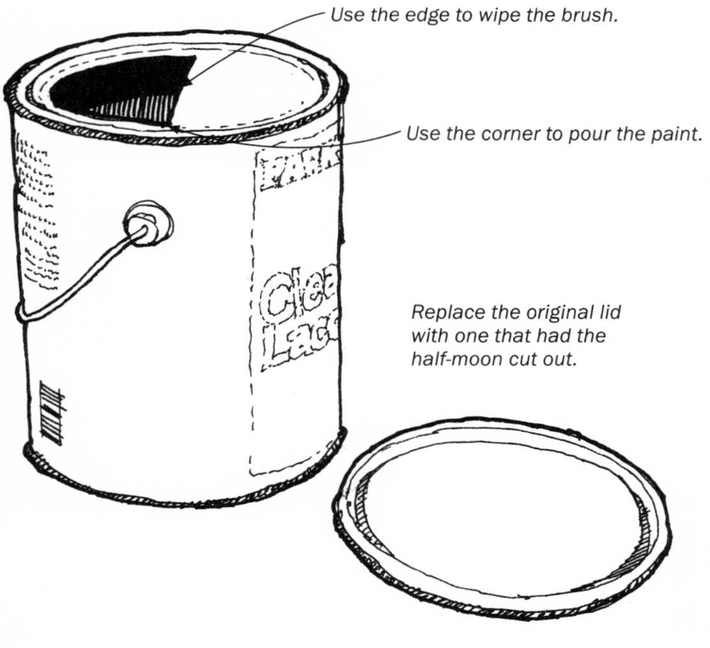

Use the edge to wipe the brush.
Use the corner to pour the paint.
Replace the original lid with one that had the half-moon cut out.

Keeping a Paint-Can Lip Dry—Another Way

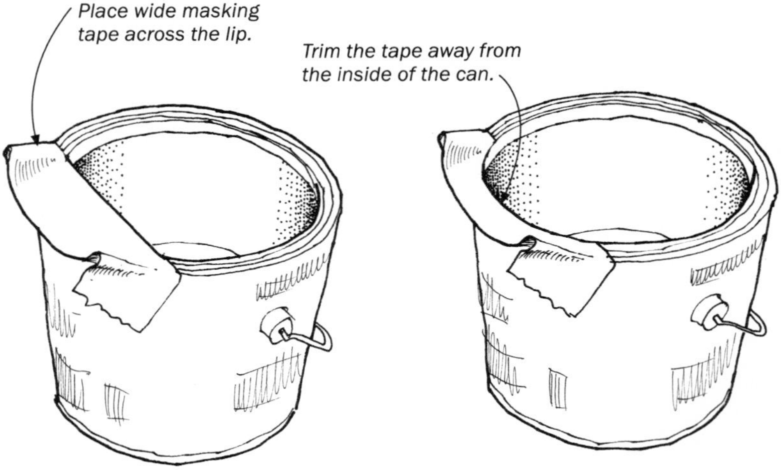
Place wide masking tape across the lip.
Trim the tape away from the inside of the can.

Remove the tape after pouring the finish.

HERE'S HOW TO KEEP VARNISH, lacquer, or paint out of the lip of often-opened cans. After wiping the lip dry, apply a piece of 2-in.-wide masking tape across the mouth of the can. Fold down the ends of the tape, as shown in the drawing above, to create a dam at the edges. Now trim the tape away from the inside of the can with a razor blade or knife. After pouring out the finish, just strip the tape off to reveal a perfectly clean lip ready for resealing.

—DANIEL A. KOBLOSH, *Redondo Beach, Calif.*

Mixing the Paint in a Long Unopened Can

WHEN A CAN OF PAINT HAS BEEN unopened for a few months, turn it upside down for a couple of days before opening. You will find when you open the can that the mixing process is almost complete.

—HERMAN J. FERSENHEIM JR., *Woodstock Valley, Conn.*

Paper Seal for Paint and Varnish Cans

OVER THE YEARS, I'VE READ SOME complicated methods for keeping a partly filled can of paint or varnish in usable condition. This method is simple and I know it works because I've used it for 30 years.

Start with a sheet of good-quality magazine paper. I use an old issue of *National Geographic.* Put the paint can lid on the paper and trace around it with a pencil. If you cut $\frac{1}{16}$ in. outside the pencil line, your paper circle will be just smaller than the inside of the can. Make sure the paper fits inside the can; if it is even a little too large, the trick won't work. Bend the paper so it can be lowered into the can, and then release it. The paper should open up flat on top of the liquid.

When you want to use the material, simply break the seal around the paper with a knife or screwdriver, remove the paper, and discard it. It's a good idea to mark the paint level on the outside of the can before resealing the lid so you won't have to shake the can and disturb the paper seal to find out how much paint you have.

—TIM HANSON, *Indianapolis, Ind.*

Keeping Paint from Skinning Over in the Can

Fumes from the solvent will displace the air in the can.

TO PREVENT A SKIN FROM FORMING on oil-based paints, carefully pour a little pool of mineral spirits or turpentine on top of the paint. Let the paint sit for a half-hour or so with the lid slightly ajar, and then tap the lid shut. The fumes from the solvent will displace the air in the can, thus preventing oxidation and paint skinning.

—C. PETER DUNCAN, *Walnut Creek, Calif.*

THE SIMPLEST METHOD OF PREVENTING paint from skinning over is to store the can upside down.

—E.W. HUNT, *Sheffield, England*

Preserving Finish with a Wine Vacuum

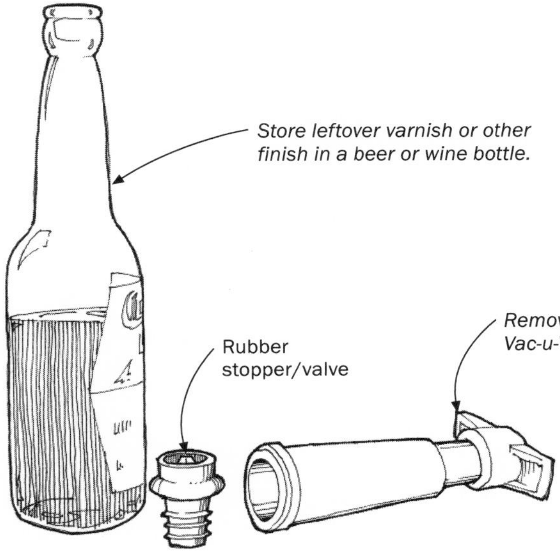
Store leftover varnish or other finish in a beer or wine bottle.
Rubber stopper/valve
Remove air with a Vac-u-Vin pump.

THE TRADITIONAL SOLUTION FOR KEEPING small leftover quantities of varnish or tung oil from skimming is to decant the finish to a smaller container to minimize the air space. Another approach, which is just as effective, is to transfer the varnish to a wine or beer bottle and apply a vacuum. Systems for evacuating the air from a wine bottle, such as Vac-u-Vin, cost less than $15 and combine a rubber stopper/valve with a hand pump.

Before using the pump, clean and rinse the bottle, and put it in a microwave for a minute to dry it out. Transfer the leftover varnish to the bottle, insert the stopper, give it eight to 10 strokes, and then label and date the bottle.

—DAVE ROBINSON, *Ann Arbor, Mich.*

Preventing Spontaneous Combustion of Oily Rags

TO AVOID SPONTANEOUS COMBUSTION, some woodworkers mistakenly seal oily rags in a glass jar with a screw top to exclude most of the air. I'm uncertain about the safety of this glass-jar and oily-rag storage system. Even inside the jar, wadded-up, oil-soaked rags contain the three ingredients needed for spontaneous combustion: an ignition source, fuel, and oxygen.

For an oil to change from a liquid to a solid, it must first absorb oxygen from the atmosphere. This oxygen absorption phase takes several hours, which accounts for the long drying time associated with oil finishes. Once sufficient oxygen has been absorbed, an exothermic (heat-producing) reaction begins. Normally, this heat dissipates harmlessly into the surrounding atmosphere as the oil dries.

When trapped inside a ball of oil-soaked rags, however, the heat produced by this reaction feeds on itself—often with disastrous results. A basic rule of chemistry is that the higher the temperature of a chemical reaction, the faster it proceeds. The heat trapped inside the rag ball causes the reaction rate to increase, producing more heat, which increases the reaction rate, which produces more heat and so on. Eventually, enough heat is produced to ignite the oily rag ball—spontaneous combustion.

Avoiding disaster is easy. Don't store oil-soaked rags in your shop. I spread my oil-soaked rags on my shop floor or across a lumber pile to dry. Once they are dry, I either toss them in the regular trash or keep them for reuse as oil-applicator rags.

—CHRIS MINICK, *Stillwater, Minn.,*
from a question by Frederick Trapp, Pinhalzinho, Brazil

Homemade Tack Rags

I'VE EXPERIMENTED WITH DIFFERENT recipes for making tack rags over the years and have used everything from linseed oil to varnish to make sticky rags that pick up dust. The recipe below is what I use now and comes pretty close to the commercial rags sold in paint stores.

Dissolve 2 oz. to 3 oz. of rosin in 1 qt. of denatured alcohol. Rosin is available from Olde Mill Cabinet Shoppe (717-755-8884). Take some cheesecloth or other type of lint-free, loose-weave cotton cloth and squirt a few thimblefuls of the dissolved rosin solution onto the cloth. Work it into the rag with your hands. Fold the cloth and store it in a resealable plastic bag to keep it from drying out.

—JEFF JEWITT, *Royalton, Ohio,*
from a question by Patrick Bates, Irving, Tex.

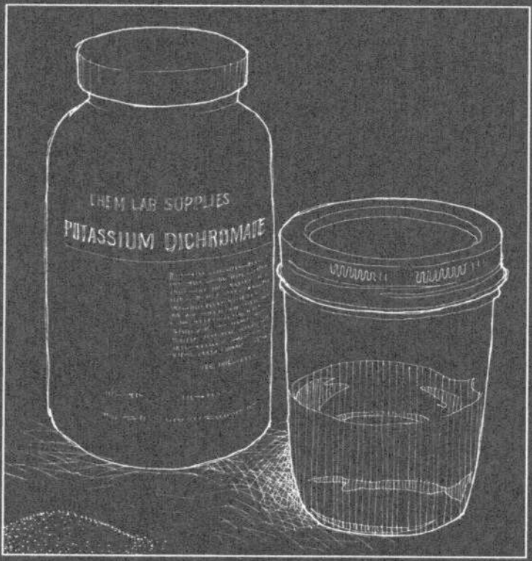
CHEM LAB SUPPLIES
POTASSIUM DICHROMATE

Chapter 5

COLORING WOOD

Dyes vs. Stains

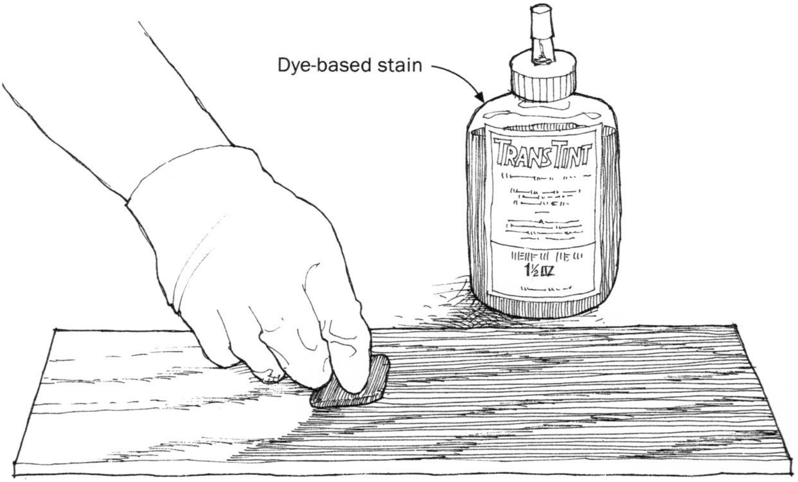

MANY WOODWORKERS are confused as to the attributes of stains and dyes and the relative advantages of each in coloring woods. Let's clear up some of the confusion. In this country, the generally accepted definition of a stain is any material that imparts color to wood without completely obscuring the wood underneath. This distinguishes stains from paints, whose function is to cover up the wood. There are three types of stains used to color wood: pigment-based, dye-based, and chemical stains.

Pigment-based stains suspend pigment, a coloring agent, in a carrier/binder solution. The binder adheres the pigment particles to the wood, and the carrier thins the mixture to allow even distribution of the pigment particles over the wood's surface. Because of their size, the pigment particles remain on the surface of the wood, lodging in pores and sanding scratches. Another result of the relatively large size of the pigment particles is that they reflect a good deal of visible light, somewhat obscuring the grain beneath them.

Dye-based stains are organic compounds that dissolve in a carrier: water, alcohol, or another organic solvent (such as mineral spirits, naphtha, or turpentine). The coloring particles are dissolved, so they're very small—about 1,000 times smaller than pigment particles. This allows them to penetrate deeply into the cellular structure of the wood, coloring it from within. Because they're smaller than the shortest wavelength of visible light, they transmit light, unlike pigment particles. This is why dye-based stains are characterized as transparent.

Chemical stains color wood by reacting with chemicals naturally present in the wood. They act more like dyes. Chemicals used to color wood include sodium hydroxide (lye), potassium dichromate, and ammonium hydroxide (ammonia). Strong acids like nitric and sulfuric also produce color changes.

Pigment-based stains are always sold premixed and are identified by the directions on the can. Because the pigments always settle to the bottom, the instructions generally tell you to stir thoroughly. Pigment-based stains are the most commonly available form of wood stain and are found in just about any hardware or paint store.

Dye-based stains are usually sold in dry powder form and are identified by the solvent in which they dissolve best. Most woodworking-supply mail-order companies sell both water-soluble and alcohol-soluble dye stains. Alcohol-soluble stains are best applied with spray equipment because they dry so quickly. Water-soluble dye stains dry more slowly, making them easier to work with. They can be applied with a brush, a rag, or with spray equipment.

A premixed stain, known as a non-grain-raising (NGR) stain, is also available. NGR stains are either alcohol- or water-soluble dyes dissolved in a blend of organic solvents designed to minimize grain raising. These dyes are very lightfast and are what the large furniture factories use. Like alcohol-soluble dye stains, however, they dry very quickly, so they are best applied with spray equipment.

Dye-stain powders and NGR stains are manufactured by H. Behlen and Bros., a division of Mohawk Finishing Products Inc. (4715 State Highway 30, Amsterdam, NY 12010-9204; 800-545-0047).

Water-, alcohol-, and oil-soluble dye-stain powders are available from W. D. Lockwood and Co. (81-83 Franklin St., New York, NY 10013; 212-966-4046). Lockwood also sells to many mail-order catalog companies that repackage the dyes under their own labels.

If you have trouble finding dye-stain powders, call one of these companies to find a local retailer.

—JEFF JEWITT, *North Royalton, Ohio, from a question by Tom Naughton, Williamsville, N.Y.*

Identifying Sanding Scratches

STAIN WILL COLLECT in sanding scratches that have been overlooked, darkening them more than the surrounding wood. If you wipe the wood with mineral spirits first, it will show up the scratches long enough for you to resand. Even if there are no scratches, wetting and wiping is a good way to remove sawdust (which is what I was doing when I discovered this trick).

—G. THEODORE ODOM, *Angleton, Tex.*

Dyeing Oak Bright Colors

TO DYE OAK, or any hardwood, a bright, deep color like blue or green or black I'd recommend using one of the three kinds of aniline dyes: water-, oil-, or alcohol-soluble. All three should be available in a well-stocked paint store, though you may have to special-order them. Some dyes can be bought mail-order from H. Behlen and Bros. (see address and phone on the facing page). All of these dyes can be brushed or wiped on, or sprayed on with the pump-type sprayer used for insecticides.

Water-soluble aniline stains are the most lightfast. In a plastic or glass container, mix about 4 oz. of dry stain powder in a 1 gal. of hot water, allow it to cool, and strain it through a triple layer of fine cheesecloth or muslin. Vary the application rate to get the color you want. Water-soluble aniline stains should be freshly prepared for each application, and they shouldn't be stored in metal containers.

Alcohol-soluble aniline stains will produce bright colors, but they are likely to be light-fugitive, especially the reds. To mix them, add 2 oz. to 6 oz. of powder to 1 gal. of a mixture composed of eight parts methanol and two parts denatured alcohol.

Oil-soluble aniline dye mixtures can be made by mixing 2 oz. to 6 oz. of stain powder to a 1 gal. of toluol, xylol, or any other aromatic petroleum solvent. Agitate the mixture well, let it settle, strain it, and apply as above. Avoid breathing the vapors from this mixture and don't work around open flames—the solution is extremely flammable. To bring out the colors of any of these dyes, especially the blacks, you may need to add a top coat of semigloss or gloss lacquer or reduced white shellac.

—OTTO HEUER, *Waukegan, Ill.,*
from a question by Kurt Martinson, Coeur d'Alene, Idaho

Coloring Tung-Oil Varnish

YOU CAN USE ARTIST'S oil colors to color tung oil and other oil-based varnishes. Artist's oil colors are simply pigments ground in linseed oil. You can buy them in tubes at an art supply store. If you add too much of the pigments to a glossy tung oil varnish, however, you'll reduce the gloss. This is especially noticeable with any of the earth colors (yellow ocher, raw umber, burnt sienna, etc.) because their pigment particles are opaque. Some of the modern pigments such as alizarin crimson and thalo blue contain vivid dyes that allow deep colors with good transparency. Buy top-grade paint, not student-grade (which is stretched with various fillers) and you'll get the best results. I usually pour a small amount of the clear varnish into a small paper cup and add the color pastes. I always experiment on scrap wood to make sure the color is right.

—OTTO HEUER, *Waukegan, Ill.,*
from a question by George M. Elrod, Huntsville, Ala.

Coloring Shellac

HERE'S HOW TO COLOR SHELLAC with dye or pigment. Mix about ½ oz. of alcohol-soluble aniline dye in a quart of denatured alcohol to make a base solution. Then make a dilute dye by adding one part base solution to three parts denatured alcohol. Mix this diluted dye with an equal amount of 3-lb.-cut shellac. I like to add a pinch of raw umber or burnt umber pigment, such as Benjamin Moore Universal Tinting Colors (UTCs) to tone down the dye. Mix the shellac well.

Apply the colored shellac with a 2½-in. or 3-in. natural-bristle brush. Fill one-third of the brush with colored shellac and tap off the excess against the side of the container. Lay on a thin coat by simply pulling the brush across the surface from one end to the other (left to right). Don't brush back and forth. You can go back over the stroke to even it off but remember to always brush in the same direction. Continue across the piece going from left to right, evening off as you go. Remember that shellac sets up quickly and you must not hesitate. Allow each coat to dry thoroughly before applying the next. Two to three coats of colored shellac will give you a nice translucent finish. If you've stained the piece prior to applying the shellac, be sure that the stain has had ample time to dry.

If you end up with streaks you're probably adding too much dye or pigment to the shellac, but the streaks could also be caused by your application technique.

—BEAU BELAJONAS, *Camden, Maine,*
from a question by John Viarengo, Downingtown, Pa.

Transparent Glaze

ALTHOUGH I WOULDN'T recommend it as a general practice, you can darken molding that has already been finished by applying a glaze over the finish. With this technique you can control the amount of color and transparency.

First, you need to mix up a glaze medium from one part varnish, one part mineral spirits or turpentine, and one-eighth part boiled linseed oil. To make a brown fruitwood color, for example, I'd use raw sienna and burnt umber, which can be bought as universal colored pigments, oil colors, or Japan colors (available from Woodfinishing Enterprises, 1729 N. 68th St., Wauwatosa, WI 53213). Add a bit of raw sienna and a touch of burnt umber to your glaze medium, keeping track of proportions. Start with small amounts—you can always add more. Mix up what you think is the color you're looking for and test it on a small section of your Deft-covered molding. Let it stand for five minutes, then gently rub with the grain. If the color isn't dark enough, add more pigment.

Once you've reached the right consistency, make up a bigger batch and you're ready for application. The basic technique for applying a glaze is to brush it on, let it stand for five minutes, then gently rub it off. Try to rub in one direction. If the glaze pulls too much or seems to drag, add a little linseed oil. Let the glaze dry overnight.

The next day, after the glaze is dry, give it a coat of satin varnish tinted with a bit of burnt umber. This evens the glaze and gives the finish more depth.

—BEAU BELAJONAS, *Camden, Maine,*
from a question by R. Winkleblock, Arroyo Grande, Calif.

Color Matching Veneer to Air-Dried Stock

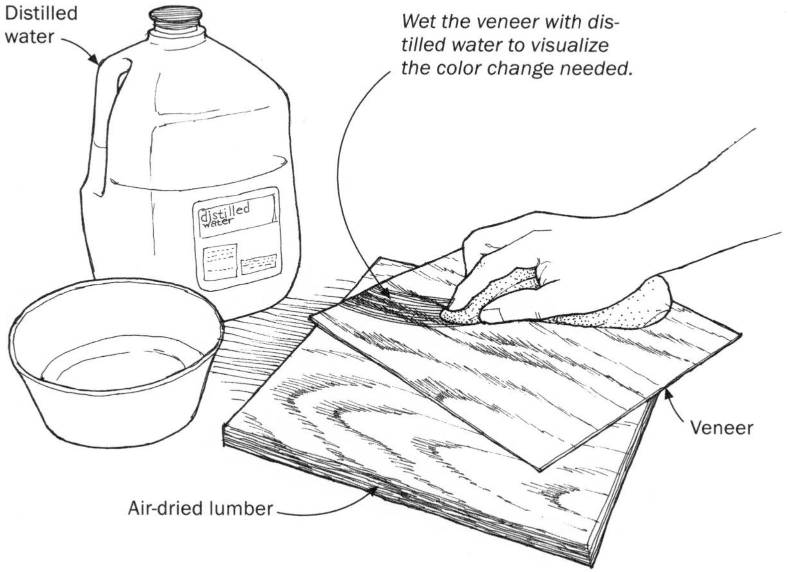
Distilled water
distilled water
Wet the veneer with distilled water to visualize the color change needed.
Veneer
Air-dried lumber

WHEN YOU COMBINE VENEER and solid wood on a piece of furniture and you can't seem to match up the color between the two, you're probably looking at the difference between air-dried and kiln-dried wood. Take walnut for example. Air-dried walnut is a deeper chocolate color, with reddish undertones, and kiln-dried walnut is usually much cooler in color, with grayish undertones. Veneer is much like kiln-dried lumber, but it is lighter in color because it has been boiled for as long as five days before slicing.

The color of the veneer can be matched to the rest of the chair using water- and alcohol-soluble dyes. This is the technique we use in our restoration business. Remember that the best results in matching a color are by using a layering technique. Build to the color you are trying to match in layers of color rather than trying to hit the color all in one shot. First, to better visualize the color you need to duplicate, wet a veneer sample and the air-dried sample with distilled water.

When the wood has dried begin to apply finish, sealer first then top coat, beginning with the sample of air-dried wood. After that it is a matter of finalizing the color of the veneer to the finished piece. I like to use shellac as the sealer because alcohol-soluble dyes mix in well and allow me to shade coats for the final color match. Often you can get just the color you want by darkening the shellac. Another way would be to add a dark-brown, alcohol-soluble dye to orange shellac. You can then top coat the veneer with the finish that you used on the air-dried part of the furniture. If you choose an oil-based varnish, shellac, or lacquer, be sure to allow for a slight deepening of color from the finish. You'll probably need to experiment on lots of scraps to get the feel for this technique.

Alcohol- and water-soluble dyes and shellac are available from a number of companies, including Woodcraft (210 Wood County Industrial Park, P.O. Box 1686, Parkersburg, WV 26102-1686; 800-225-1153) and Garrett Wade (161 Avenue of the Americas, New York, NY 10013; 800-221-2942).

—JEFF JEWITT, *North Royalton, Ohio, from a question by F.W. Feekin, Taylors, S.C.*

Bringing Out Maple's Depth with Danish Oil

TO BRING OUT THE GRAIN and depth of maple, the best approach is to use a water-soluble dye stain first, which will even out tonal disparities and establish the undertone of color that your want. Next I would seal the wood with a Danish oil, which will "kick up" any curl figure and enhance surface luster and shimmer. You can then finish with the top coat of your choice, though I'd advise a barrier coat of shellac if you're using a water-based finish.

For more color, you can add a gel stain any time after the wood has been sealed with Danish oil—this is technically called glazing. You can manipulate the amount and the way you wipe the excess off to achieve specific effects. For example, by leaving more in crevices and corners, you can simulate age and patina. I'd advise against starting out with a gel stain, however, which will not bring out the depth or accentuate any curl figure in the maple.

—JEFF JEWITT, *North Royalton, Ohio,*
from a question by Derek Sedillo, Torrance, Calif.

Using Potassium Dichromate

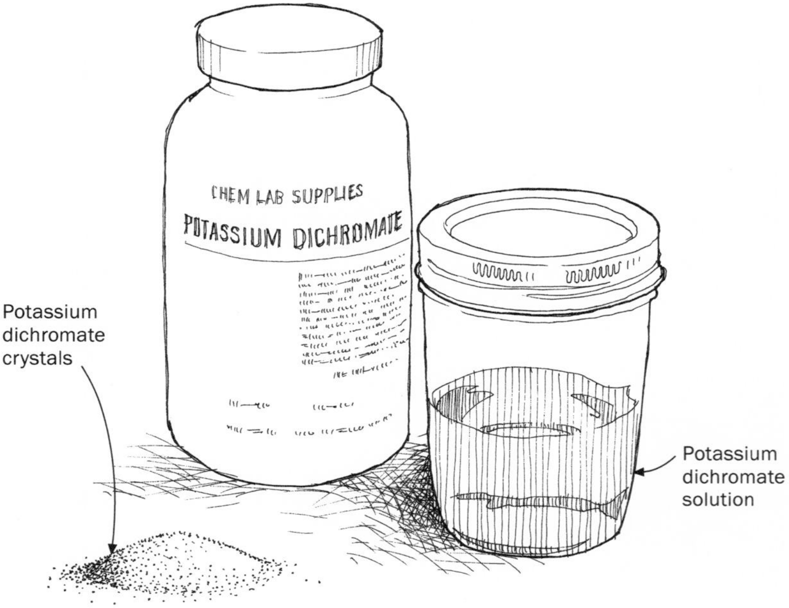

POTASSIUM DICHROMATE is a traditional wood-finishing chemical that has been used over the years to darken cherry and other woods. It is usually sold in the crystal state and mixed with water to make a concentrated solution. The chemical isn't really a stain but a dye. To my knowledge it is perfectly harmless to the wood. On woods with no tannic acid, it may convey its own yellow-orange hue; on woods with tannic acid, such as oak, potassium dichromate can produce a great variety of colors. When using it, be sure to work in a room with good ventilation and wear eye protection and gloves.

—GEORGE FRANK, *South Venice, Fla., from a question by E. Jeff Justis, Memphis, Tenn.*

Using Potassium Dichromate to Produce a Brown Finish on Cherry

THE NATURAL COLOR OF CHERRY as it ages, even under a clear finish, is more red than brown. However, a brown finish may be desirable and can be obtained on properly sanded wood as follows.

After sponging with lukewarm water, resand with 6/0 (or well-worn 0000) garnet paper, and apply an even coat of potassium dichromate in a very dilute water solution, about the color of weak tea. This oxidizes the tannic acid in the wood; when quite dry, the cherry will have a brownish, rather rusty appearance. For a deeper shade, repeat the process or use a stronger solution the first time.

Prepare a finely ground paste wood filler just as one would do for an open-grained wood (even cherry has pores that should be filled for a first-class finish) and add burnt umber or burnt sienna in oil, not enough to try to stain the wood, which would result in a muddy appearance, but just enough to tone the cherry on the brown side; the real color is already in the wood from the dichromate, and more burnt umber than sienna will bring out the brown shades.

Over the completely dry coat of filler, none of which will remain on the surface when properly rubbed off across the grain, brush on an even coat of one of the new satin or low-luster polyurethane varnishes with a fine-hair sable brush of 1½-in. size. Modern satin varnishes can be applied very easily and do not have the tendency to lap, but flatten out beautifully in an hour or so in a dust-free room. Of course, a gloss varnish can be used and rubbed with pumice and oil if one wishes. The modern non-grain-raising stains do not require the additional work of sponging and sanding, but they don't produce the clear and nonfading results of some of the older methods.

—EDWARD L. DEPUY, *Black Mountain, N.C.*

Acquiring and Using Potassium Dichromate

TO FIND SMALL QUANTITIES of potassium dichromate crystals, first try companies listed under "Laboratory Equipment and Supplies" in the Yellow pages. They are more likely to deal in small quantities than companies listed under "Chemicals." If your phone book doesn't have these listings, try asking the local high school for the name of the company that supplies the chemistry lab. If you can't find a nearby source, a company that will sell small quantities of potassium dichromate crystals by mail is Chem Lab Supplies (13814 Inglewood Ave., Hawthorne, CA 90250; www.chemlab.com). Potassium dichromate is also available under the name bichromate of potash from Garrett Wade (161 Avenue of the Americas, New York, NY 10213; www.garrettwade.com).

There is also confusion about the safety of using potassium dichromate. Dr. Michael McCann, of the Art Hazards Information Center in New York City, says it can cause skin ulcers and severe allergic reactions. He advises wearing goggles and rubber gloves when using it. Some chemical suppliers say that selling the chemical to hobbyists is forbidden by Food and Drug Administration regulations, but an FDA spokesman said that potassium dichromate—neither food nor drug—doesn't come under its jurisdiction. One chemical salesman said companies who sell industrial chemicals in large quantities are often reluctant to sell to hobbyists because they might hurt themselves and sue. Many companies also find it easier and cheaper to sell only 100-lb. sacks or boxcar loads.

For those who plan to experiment with potassium dichromate, dissolve 50 grams of potassium dichromate crystals in a half-liter of (preferably) rainwater to make a concentrated solution. Keep this in a bottle and experiment on scrap wood with more dilute solutions. To start, take another half-liter of water and add to it two-tenths of your concentrated dichromate. Saturate the wood. Take up the excess liquid with a well-squeezed sponge and let the wood dry thoroughly, for half a day at least. Then check how close you are from your goal. Be patient and know that the greater part of wood finishing is experimenting.

—GEORGE FRANK, *South Venice, Fla., and others*

Recipe for Fake Antiques

PROPER PLANNING of inlaid work excludes the use of stain or dye. However, there are exceptions. In France in the 1920s I worked with others in an assembly-line situation producing "antiques," most of which were inlaid. Each manufacturer of these fakes had his own mixture of dye, mainly a mixture of potassium dichromate and muriatic acid. This dye imitated the natural fading of all the woods and sort of blended them together. When dry, we fine-sanded each piece and then washed it with a brew of strong tea, which gave a pleasant yellowish hue to the object. The goal here was to meld all the colors together.

Unless this is your goal, too, my advice is to select all the woods when doing inlay work so that no staining or dyeing is required after assembly.

—GEORGE FRANK, *South Venice, Fla., from a question by George Rives*

Alkanet Root in Linseed Oil

MANY YEARS AGO a cabinetmaker showed me how to kill off the strange color overtones that you sometimes get by using potassium dichromate on mahogany or pine. After steeling the treated surface, flood on a solution of alkanet root in linseed oil. The alkanet root is a woody, granular material that has a rich red dye in the fibers. This material is soluble in oil but not in water. I put about a handful in a one-quart mayonnaise jar, and then fill it almost full with linseed oil. After this sets for a few days, with an occasional shaking, it can be flooded on the dry treated wood and then the surplus wiped off in an hour.

All of the fibers lifted by the water in the oxidizing solution should be removed by steel wool.

The general effect is to highlight the grain and give a deep look to any subsequent finish, but the best part is the elimination of the unwanted color.

—ROBERT H. DEERING, *Harrison, Maine*

Sources for Alkanet Root

IF YOU ARE SEARCHING for but can't find alkanet root, an old-time orange-red stain, you can get the color you want with oil-soluble aniline dyes, which can be dissolved in oil, lacquer, thinner, or turpentine. However, if you insist on alkanet root, your best bet would be to shop in herb stores. Specify the Latin name of the plant, which is *Alkanna tinctoria.* You may be able to get the root or the dye extracted from it. Alkanet root is also available in small quantities from Kremer Pigments (228 Elizabeth St., New York, NY 10012; 212-219-2394). Kremer also carries several other hard-to-find pigments, organic stains, resins, and waxes.

—GEORGE FRANK, *South Venice, Fla., from a question by James B. Patrick*

Staining Curly Maple

CURLY MAPLE—FIDDLEBACK, tiger-tail, or whatever you may call it—requires a staining technique all its own. Maple with a curl was the favorite wood for the stocks of the muzzle-loading rifles of yesteryear. The staining method described here has come down by word of mouth from the old gunsmiths.

Great-grandpa used two stains and he made both of them. For the first you must find a handful of rusty cut nails—very old and very rusty cut nails are best. Place about a dozen in a soup bowl and cover them with homemade apple-cider vinegar, the stronger the better. Do not use a metal dish and do not substitute synthetic vinegar or white vinegar. Cover to prevent evaporation and let stand for two weeks.

For the second stain dissolve potassium dichromate crystals in water. It need not be a saturated solution but I use it fairly strong. You can buy these crystals, or you might try begging a few from your high-school chemistry teacher. This stain can be used immediately.

We will assume your curly maple stock is now in the white and you have it sanded dead smooth. Use a rag swab to coat the stock with the vinegar stain. When it dries it should be about the color of a slate roof—not very pretty. This stain will penetrate deeply into the soft spots, but it will only sit on the surface of the hard stripes. Allow an hour for drying, or speed it up a bit with some heat. Now with a good grade of 220 garnet paper, sand this stain off the hard stripes; you will be unable to sand it off the soft spots where it has penetrated deeply. Sand a bit more here and bit less there to bring out all the figure. Be sure to use a sanding block. The stripes are very hard and the spaces are soft, so sanding without a block can result in a washboard effect.

Now, using a new swab, stain the stock with potassium dichromate stain. This stain will penetrate those hard, white stripes and color them a rich orange-yellow. It will also change that slate color to a rich dark brown. When the second stain is dry, sand it off with a very fine paper, Now put several drops of boiled linseed oil in the palm of each hand and rub it in lovingly, lean back, and feast your eye. The oil is only to bring out the color. Allow plenty of drying time before you apply your favorite finish.

If you prefer to stick to grandpa's methods, give it an oil finish. An old gunsmith put it this way: "...three drops of boiled linseed oil and then three weeks of rub." Use as little oil as possible to cover the stock.

—BOB WINGER, *Montoursville, Pa.*

Recipe for Walnut-Colored Stain

HERE'S A RECIPE for a traditional walnut-colored stain. First dissolve walnut crystals (also called cassel extract or Vandyke crystals) in warm water. The more concentrated the solution is, the darker your color will be. This dye will have more penetrating power if you add to it some commercial ammonia (about 1 pint to 1 gal. of dye), or some soda ash, also called washing soda or sal soda (about 3 oz. to 1 gal. of dye), or some lye (about ½ teaspoon to 1 gal. of dye). Of the three, ammonia is the best for general use. Walnut crystals are available from Garrett Wade (161 Avenue of the Americas, New York, NY 10213; www.garrettwade.com) under the name Vandyke crystals.

—GEORGE FRANK, *South Venice, Fla.,*
from a question by T. Smith, Washington, D.C.

Shoe-Polish Stain

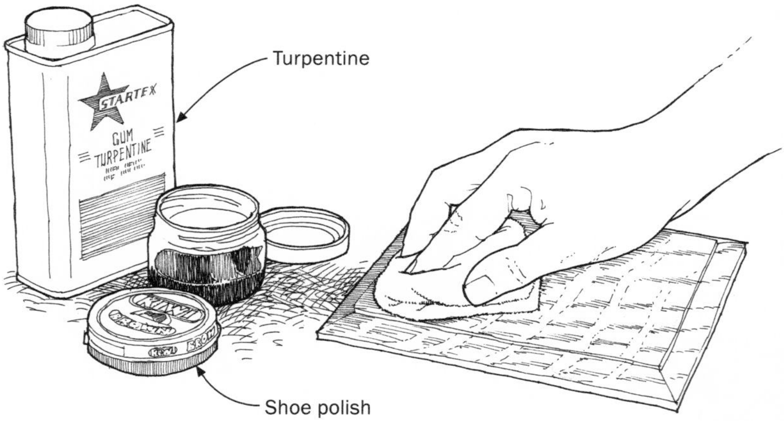

ORDINARY WAX-BASED shoe polish makes a good stain and filler for open-grained woods such as walnut and oak. In a small jar, mix a chunk of polish with enough turpentine to liquefy, then rub the liquid in and wipe off as you would with regular stain. Several shades are available—I like the black with walnut. The coating won't interfere with subsequent finishing.

—CARL R. VITALE

Two Honey-Tan Stain Recipes

HERE ARE TWO good honey-tan stains. The first is perfect for pine because it doesn't darken the end grain more than the surface. Buy a bag of chewing tobacco and soak it overnight in a quart jar filled half-and-half with ammonia and water. Decant it and it's ready to apply. Because the stain is weak, I use 10 to 12 applications, but I can do three applications on a winter evening. The stain is transparent and unaffected by subsequent wetting. It raises the grain, so I steel-wool after every three or four coats. For a final finish, I generally use wax or urethane.

My other finish formula apparently only works with maple. I oil the wood with bacon fat and place it in my barbecue smoker with a small green twig in one corner. After half an hour the maple turns brown-black. Wipe it clean and seal with linseed oil. I tried this with pine and it turned a horrible yellow color, so I conclude that maple darkens through chemical action.

—P. L. LaMontagne, *New Britten, Pa.*

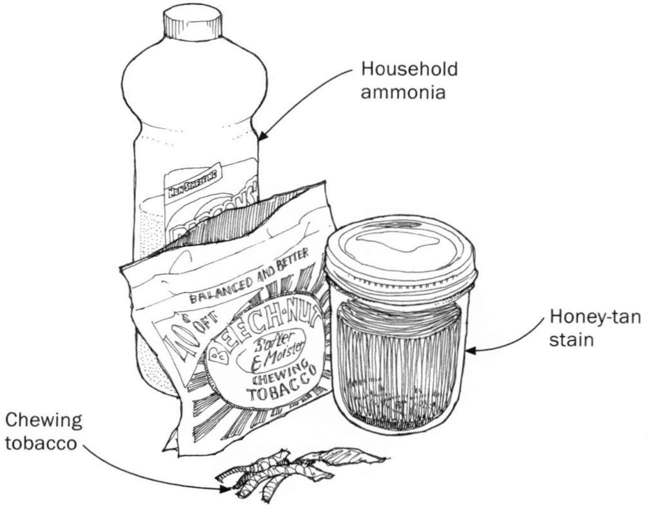

Several Suggestions for Aging Cedar

Wash the wood with the solution to produce a weathered look.
Ferrous sulfate
FERROUS SULFATE

HERE'S A METHOD for producing a weathered look on cedar that works well and is less caustic than lye. Mix about 1 to 1½ tablespoons of ferrous sulfate (a lawn fertilizer available at most nurseries) in a gallon of water and wash the wood with this solution. Expose the wood to sunlight until the desired color is achieved. As I recall, it takes days, not weeks, to work.

—DARYL PROCTOR, *Santa Fe, N.M.*

HERE'S HOW TO achieve the silver gray color of cedar that has aged in the weather. Begin by soaking the cedar in a concentrated solution of lye before you cut the frame parts to final size. This will wash out all the sap and chemical impurities in the wood; using a stiff brush with the lye will speed this up, but protect your hands with rubber gloves and wear eye protection. Wash off the lye with clear water and let the wood dry slowly. Then expose the wood to sunlight or even a suntan lamp for as long as possible, weeks or even months if you can.

Next coat the wood with freshly slaked lime and then remove all the lime you can with a soft brush. Bleach the wood several times (Clorox is fine), drying it in between treatments. Before applying the final finish, neutralize any bleach that remains with a strong solution of vinegar. This process is long and tedious but worth the effort.

—GEORGE FRANK, *South Venice, Fla.,*
from a question by Lewis S. Farinholt, Kenner, La.

TO ACHIEVE A WEATHERED LOOK, paint cedar with a strong solution of tea and let the wood dry. Make a solution of ferrous sulfate (available from Chem Lab Supplies, 13814 Inglewood Ave., Hawthorne, CA 90250; www.chemlab.com), about one teaspoon per cup of water, and apply it to the wood. The darkness of the gray can be changed by repeated applications or by changing the strengths of the solutions.

—N. H. CEAGLSKE, *Minneapolis, Minn.*

HEY, YOU COULD just let the wood weather outdoors. In New England, cedar shingles take about three years to turn from brown to silvery gray.

—LARRY GREEN, *Bethel, Conn.*

Walnut-Husk Stain

A WONDERFUL WOOD STAIN can be made from walnut husks. In France the famous concoction was called *brou de noix* (literally, brew of walnut), the pet dye of all old-time French *ébenistes*. Since those days *brou de noix* has been replaced by far better and easier-to-use aniline dyes. Still, maybe *brou de noix* has a nostalgic value and charm that some of us can still detect. Here's how we made the stuff into a wonderful stain.

The boss lady soaked the walnuts' green husks (not the hard brown shells or the edible fruit) in rainwater for a few days and then she put this muck over a slow fire, being careful not to let it boil. All the while, her hands became pleasantly brown. She added some soda ash (dry sodium carbonate) while brewing, approximately a heaping teaspoon per gallon, and let the brew simmer for two or three days. And that was it. She let it cool, strained it through an old linen cloth (burlap would work just as well), and then filled green bottles with the filtered liquid. She kept the bottles firmly sealed and in a dark area until we were ready to use our *brou de noix*.

If you insist on using alcohol, don't put it into the brew but into the brewmaster. Rye would do, but go easy.

—GEORGE FRANK, *South Venice, Fla.,*
from a question by Wesley Kobylak, Tuscarora, N.Y.

Coal Tar Stain

An old recipe for an inexpensive brown wood stain calls for a mixture of asphaltum and kerosene. The asphaltum (also known as coal tar or asphalt) supplies the color, and the kerosene is merely a solvent. There are two drawbacks. One is that the stain never hardens permanently or polymerizes as it ages and can always be dissolved by an organic solvent. The result is that the subsequent application of a lacquer or varnish will lift the stain and thereby lighten the wood. It will work as a stain, but it's a trifle difficult to get the exact color desired. The other drawback is kerosene's qualities as a solvent. I'd recommend using mineral spirits instead, which dries much more quickly and more dependably than kerosene.

To make the stain, obtain asphalt from a hardware store: a small can of asphalt roofing or gutter paint, without any fillers or additives, will do. Then add a teaspoon of asphalt paint in two or three ounces of paint thinner. Try it on a scrap of wood, thinning or thickening the mixture to get lighter or deeper shades. When you have the color you want, brush it on in fairly wet coats, let it soak in, and lightly dry the surface with a paper towel. After an hour or two, you can apply the finish—a good satin varnish is a safe choice.

—Don Newell, *Farmington, Mich.,*
from a question by Peggy Gefellers, Greenville, Tenn.

Using Ferrous Sulfate to Bring Out the Grain in Maple

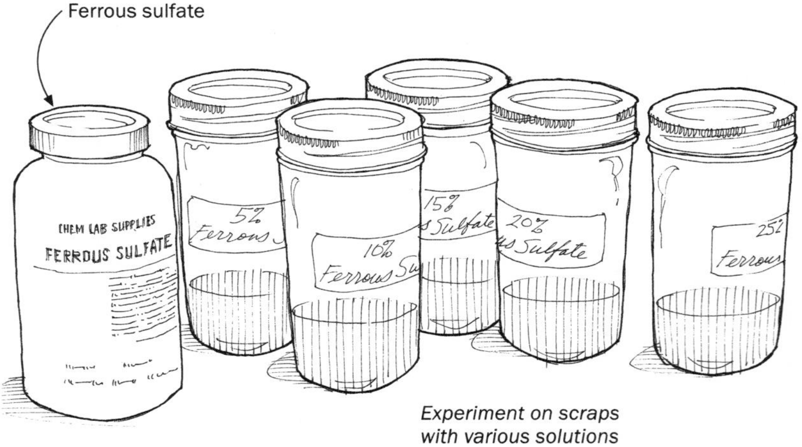

Experiment on scraps with various solutions from 5% to 25%.

THERE ARE MANY BEAUTIFUL, deep, dramatic, and vivid colors in every piece of wood, which, like the sleeping princess in the fairy tale, are just waiting to be awakened. Many woods, such as oak, contain tannic acid that reacts when various chemicals, such as ammonia, are applied to the surface. The chemical reaction that takes place changes the wood's color. The reaction between bird's-eye maple and ferrous sulfate is similar. However, one difficulty in pinpointing the exact mixture that will bring out the desired result is that some maples react more intensely to the chemical than others. One maple species called palazota, found in the Balkan region of Europe, reacts much more readily to contact with ferrous sulfate than many of our domestic maple species.

So, in lieu of any definite formula, I suggest you carry out the following experiments on scraps of the same wood that you are using on your project. This will help you find the best mixture of sulfate and water to get the results you desire. First, put 100 grams (about 1½ oz.) of rain or distilled water in each of five clean glass containers or tumblers. Next, mix 5 grams of ferrous sulfate into the first glass, 10 grams into the second, 15 grams into the third, 20 grams into the fourth, and 25 grams into the fifth (1 gram equals .035 oz., dry weight). Stir each with a clean stick until dissolved. You have now 5%, 10%, 15%, 20%, and 25% solutions of ferrous sulfate. Keep the glasses covered to prevent contamination.

Now, using a clean rubber sponge (a new one for each mixture), apply each solution to a different scrap of maple, prepared identically (sanded, scraped, etc.) as the wood for your project. With a squeezed-out sponge, wipe off the extra liquid, and let each sample dry in the shade at room temperature. Number each sample, and keep a written record of every detail of your operations. One of these samples is certain to meet with your approval.

—GEORGE FRANK, *Venice, Fla.,*
from a question by Jay Davis, Austin, Tex.

What Are Universal Colors, and Where Can I Get Them?

UNIVERSAL COLORS, or more correctly universal tinting colors (UTCs), are made from pigments that are ground into a vehicle (generally a mixture of glycol either and acrylic) that is compatible with a wide variety of finishing materials, including both oil-based and water-based products and, to a lesser extent, lacquer. They are best used in water-based products. Because some of them contain water, only small amounts can be used in lacquer. They should not be used with shellac.

If you want to tint an oil finish like Watco, you can use UTCs, which are available in 1.5-oz. tubes from Highland Hardware (800-241-6748). You also can get them from most professional paint stores. Or you can use artist's oil paints or Japan colors. Both of these are available in a wider selection of colors than UTCs, and they disperse much better in the Watco. Besides that, they're generally available at your local art-supply house.

—JEFF JEWITT, *North Royalton, Ohio, from a question by Stephan Vitas, Washington, D.C.*

Color Matching with Eyebrow Pencils

FOR COLOR MATCHING in small spots, try Maybelline eyebrow pencils.

—JIM BUELL, *West Covina, Calif.*

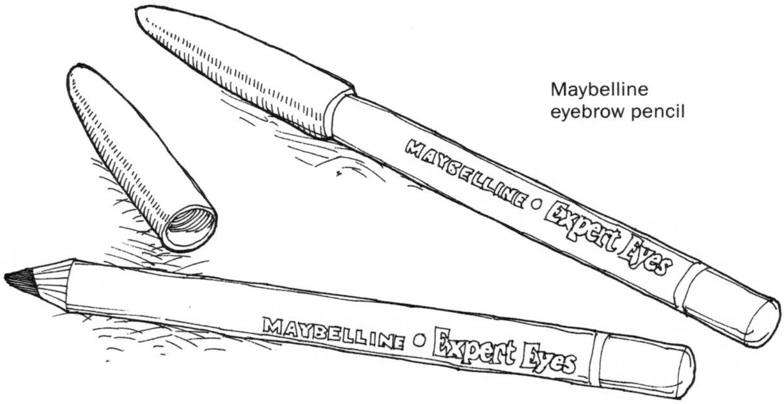

Spraying Stain

TRY APPLYING wiping stain with a spray gun. It goes on faster and more uniformly, and then wipes off with fewer rags.

—ROBERT M. VAUGHN, *Roanoke, Va.*

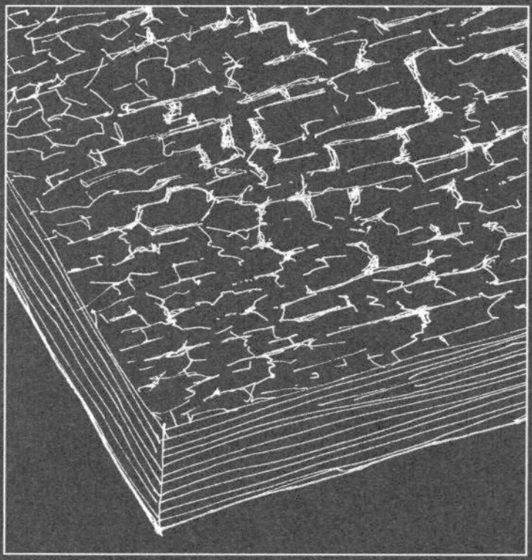

Chapter 6

SPECIALTY & CRACKED FINISHES

Staining to Accentuate the Grain in Maple

MY INTEREST IN STAINING maple began with Kentucky rifles, which are known for their curly maple and rich, 200-year-old patinas. Trying to find a commercial stain was fruitless, while the many traditional staining techniques (potassium permanganate, chromium trioxide, nitric acid with dissolved iron) were either dangerous, hard to control, or had undesirable side effects. By chance I found a supplier of pure-color liquid aniline dyes, which, after some experimentation, produced brilliant colors of great and subtle variety with all of the grain brought out. The procedure is not quick, but if you like to experiment or if you're after a color that is just right, mixing your own aniline stain may be the answer.

You begin with water-soluble aniline dye powder (available from Woodworker's Supply, 1108 North Glenn Rd., Casper, WY 82601). The powder is available in more than 50 colors and comes in a 1-oz. container. I dilute the power with five or six parts water to make a working stain.

I've used two different approaches to finding the color I want. The first is to mix various quantities of the stains, testing them on a piece of wood or paper, until I get a pleasing color. The second is to have in hand a color to match. I start experimenting with small quantities in a tiny 50-ml beaker. Guessing at a formula I think will match the original color, I measure out a small amount with an eyedropper. After the colors are all mixed, I add enough water, again with an eyedropper, to dilute the colors by five or six to one. The procedure makes very small quantities and so dilute that four to six applications are needed to build up the color. I test it on a piece of waterproof paper, first writing the formula at the top. Then, using a Q-tip, I put six to eight stripes of stain across the paper. After drying, I stain all the stripes again, except the top two. After all six to eight applications, you can compare the test stripes to the original.

You usually find that your conception of how the original color was put together is wrong. So you have to go back to the formula for an adjustment and a mix of a new test stain. This may seem tedious but it can be relatively fast. In the stain mentioned above, which I recently mixed, the total time needed was a few hours stretched over a four-day period with about 20 different stains mixed. Yet despite the fact that I made two false starts before finding the right formula, the final stain matches the original color. I was convinced the original had a touch of red in it, but indeed it did not. Once the stain is matched on the paper strip, I switch to a test piece of wood and finish it exactly like the project itself. With these procedures I have found many beautiful, unique stains, all exceptionally clear and grain-accentuating.

Final formulas may seem strange or overly complex. My recent stain has eight parts orange, two yellow, two jet black, and one brown; it produces an exquisite honey-brown color. I study my final test-stain blocks in many lights: incandescent, fluorescent, direct sunlight, north light, and subdued evening light to get the tones right. A two-stain process often heightens the figure in gunstock woods like curly maple. I apply a weak brown or black stain during the whiskering stage. A final sanding removes the stain from the hard curl and leaves it on the soft curl. Staining a second time adds the desired color to the hard curl and darkens the soft curl even more.

—LYNN FICHTER, *Harrisonburg, Va.*

Staining Curly Maple

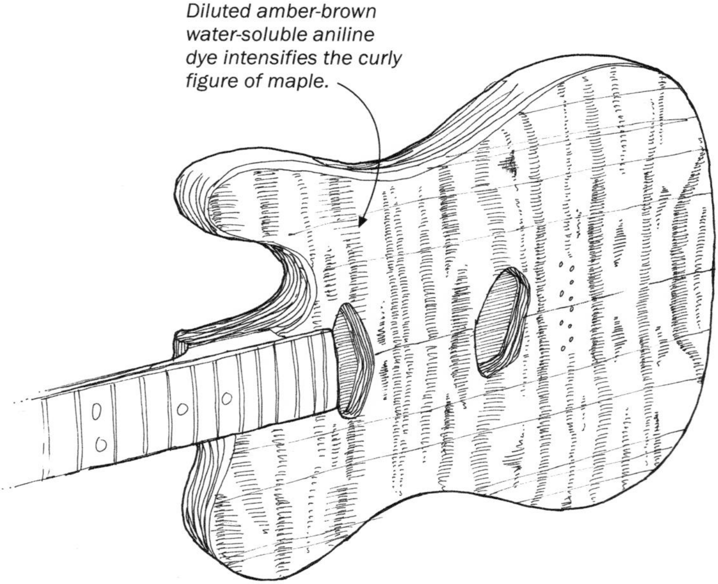
Diluted amber-brown
water-soluble aniline
dye intensifies the curly
figure of maple.

IT IS CERTAINLY POSSIBLE to intensify the curly figure of maple through staining. This is because any transparent dye applied to the raw wood will absorb more into the wavy end grain that creates the figure in curly wood than into the adjacent plain grain. This intensifies the contrast between the waves and the normal grain. For staining, I find that it is best to work with light concentrations of color, flooding the wood completely and wiping off the excess stain while it is still wet. I've gotten the best results with a water-soluble aniline dye, which will penetrate the wood the deepest, but other anilines and NGR (non-grain-raising) stains will give very acceptable results as well. However, avoid pigmented stains, as they will muddy the grain, as well as the contrast you seek to amplify. Many chemical stains will also bring out curl: copper sulfate, zinc sulfate, and ferrous sulfate enjoy favorable reputations for grain enhancement. As with aniline dyes, such chemicals will darken and change the wood's color, but, unfortunately, this usually occurs in a much less predictable way than with dyes.

Bringing out curl without darkening or adding color is somewhat more difficult. In the musical-instrument business I own, we run hundreds of curly and quilted tops for electric bass guitars each year and stain each very lightly with diluted amber-brown, water-soluble aniline dye. This works well for us—it's hard to tell that the wood has any dye on it at all. After the instruments are finished, the wood has that warm look and color of slightly aged, natural maple, but the grain fairly leaps out at you. As a result, figured maple is far and away the most popular wood for our basses.

—MICHAEL DRESDNER, *Perkasie, Pa.,*
from a question by Michael F. Gibbons, Barnstable, Mass.

Staining Maple to Bring Out the Grain

HERE'S MY RECOMMENDATION for staining and finishing a maple floor a light-brown to medium-brown color to bring out the grain. First, to accentuate the grain of maple, you must use a completely transparent stain. I would use an alcohol-based aniline stain, probably a "golden oak" color. Aniline stain is more likely to be absorbed selectively into the grain structure of the maple, thus highlighting it.

As to finishing material, Waterlox Gym Floor Finish is good and durable. Another good finish is shellac. It is surprisingly durable, unless one of your friends happens to spill straight whiskey on it.

—DON NEWELL, *Farmington, Mich.,*
from a question by James M. Harris, Chantilly, Va.

Accenting Curly Maple's Figure

THERE IS NOTHING LIKE the colonial-era golden-amber color that figured maple takes on after many years of exposure to light and to the oils of the human hand. In contrast to cherry, which oxidizes rather rapidly, maple achieves this color slowly. Trying to hasten the darkening by using stains can be frustrating. The irregular grain takes stain unevenly and too often ends up looking stained. It is understandable that it stains unevenly, considering the wildly varied orientation of the grain, to the surface. The trick, then, is to color the wood, highlight the grain, and still have it look like natural oxidation.

The process I go through is quite simple, but it takes a bit of practice and some trial and error. I apply several coats of tinted varnish instead of staining and then finishing over the stain. This process eliminates the splotchiness of staining and allows a lot of control over the color. Although most of my experience is with rock or sugar maple, these techniques will work equally well with figured red maple and many other woods.

For maximum finish clarity the wood must be properly prepared, which for me means the polished surface left by a sharp plane. Planing figured maple is a difficult task, and I frequently rely on some help from a scraper. But when done right, the surface shines.

Getting the right color to suit your taste, the wood and the overall design of the piece is the trial-and-error part of the job. I use a combination of spar varnish (synthetic varnish, such as polyurethane, seems to work equally well), boiled linseed oil, and turpentine in equal parts, to which I add the color. My favorite colorant is Minwax Golden Oak stain. For the first coat or two, I add about four tablespoons of color to a pint of the above mixture. Artist's oil pigments also work well and can be combined for subtle shadings or to get many new colors. The varnish and oil add to the pigment's golden color. For the initial coat or two, it is better to keep the color light to avoid the splotchy look from uneven absorption. Add more color as needed to subsequent coats.

I brush on the finish, let it sit until it feels tacky, and then rub the surface thoroughly to remove any excess. Although some of the color comes off, the rubbing develops a smooth finish that needs very little steel-wooling later. I build up several thin, colored layers, altering the color of the varnish as necessary. Three or four coats are usually sufficient. For extra protection, such as on a tabletop, I'll add a few coats of clear finish once the color is right. For a final coat, I apply a combination of beeswax and boiled linseed oil with a 0000 steel wool pad.

—GARRETT HACK, *Thetford Center, Vt.,*
from a question by Dan Campbell, Meyersville, N.J.

Finishing to Emphasize Figure in Tiger Maple

THE KEY TO BRINGING OUT the figure in tiger maple is to color the wood with a dye stain. Unlike pigmented stains, which cover up the wood, dye stains accentuate the subtle highlights and figure of any wood species.

I've had good success enhancing the figure of bird's-eye maple with a multistrip dye-stain process. The overall staining process is relatively simple. But like any new technique, you should practice on scraps until you are comfortable with the results. I use water-soluble dyes for staining my projects because the colors are vibrant, and they are fade resistant. Unfortunately, the water in the dye solution tends to raise the grain of the wood. For this reason, I always wet the raw wood with water during my sanding sequence to intentionally raise the fibers. After the wood has dried, I continue with my final sanding (to 220 grit on maple). Once the grain has been raised and sanded flat, it will not raise again during subsequent staining operations.

To begin the staining sequence, I first apply a dilute solution of a black, water-soluble dye to the maple. Keep the wood wet with the dye solution for about five minutes. Then wipe off the excess. Once the stained wood has thoroughly dried (usually overnight), lightly sand the entire surface with 220-grit sandpaper. Light sanding removes the black stain from the surface of the maple boards but not from the figured areas. Now I apply an antique-cherry, water-soluble dye stain to the piece. When the wood is dry, it is ready to top coat with finish.

I usually finish my pieces with a waterborne acrylic lacquer like Carver Tripp Safe-N-Simple clear finish, but before top-coating, I seal the stained wood with two coats of shellac (2-lb. cut). The shellac seal coat prevents the water in the finish from dissolving the water-soluble dyes used to color the piece. Sealing the surface is particularly important if you plan to brush on the finish coats. Three coats of finish will usually be sufficient for long-term protection and everyday use.

—CHRIS MINICK, *Stillwater, Minn.,*
from a question by Ken Drews, Phoenix, Md.

Achieving Uniform Color with Stains

APPLYING LIQUID STAIN, especially undiluted, to unsealed wood can cause uneven coloring. The reason is that different pieces of wood and even different areas of the same board can absorb colorants to a greater or lesser degree. I know of two ways to solve the problem.

The first is to brush on the stain in several applications, each one thinned down. Skip the darker areas on the following coats, and work on the lighter, less absorbent areas. Blend light and dark sections until you get a uniform color.

The second method is to seal the wood initially with thinned-down coats of finishing product (lacquer or varnish) before applying the stain. Put on the seal coat, let it stand for a few minutes, and then wipe the surface with a cloth to get it as dry as possible. Before the seal coat can harden, apply the first coat of stain. No need to thin the stain unless you want to lighten its color. Make sure that the stain and the sealer material are compatible. Water stains won't take to a surface sealed with petroleum-based varnish or oil.

—DON NEWELL, *Farmington, Mich., from a question by R. S. Nelson, Albuquerque, N.M.*

A FRIEND WAS VISITING ME when the discussion turned to how to achieve a uniform color when staining wood. He smiled and said, "If you want uniform color, paint the wood." While his remark might seem a little strong, he was not entirely wrong. A craftsman uses wood because of its endless variety of grain, markings, and color. Factories, spawning furniture on the assembly line, are concerned about uniformity. The latest, cheapest, surest, and most shameless method is to bleach the wood to a neutral, paperlike uniformity, and on top of such gelded wood build up a finish with pigmented lacquers and glazes. One may as well use wood-grained contact paper or a plastic laminate. They are always uniform.

—GEORGE FRANK, *South Venice, Fla., from a question by R. S. Nelson, Albuquerque, N.M.*

Matching Heartwood and Sapwood in Cherry

TO BLEND AND MATCH AREAS of lighter cherry sapwood into the darker heartwood, I would use two or three thin coats of a penetrating oil/pigment stain, such as those put out by Minwax. Pick the color closest to the tone of the heartwood (or buy two cans and mix your own). Apply the stain with a wad of cloth or a narrow brush, going only to the edge of the sapwood. If you run over onto the heartwood, rub or brush the color out quickly so you don't get a hard edge showing where the stain stopped. "Experimenting" involves handling the stain delicately, particularly at the edges of the sapwood, so the touched-up areas don't show. Keep in mind that when the stain dries (in about 24 hours) it will be lighter than it is when wet.

When the wood is properly colored and the stain is dry, steel-wool the surface lightly to remove any pigment residue. Then apply your finish. Minwax is an excellent material, but if you are planning to use lacquer, let the stain dry for a week before applying it. Use a thin first coat to help seal in the stain before applying full, wet coats. With varnish or oils, you need no waiting period.

—DON NEWELL, *Farmington, Mich., from a question by Ben Blackwell, Albuquerque, N.M.*

Thick, Clear, 3-D Finish for a Tabletop

THOSE HEAVY-PLASTIC, GLASS-SMOOTH coatings on restaurant tables are probably either a non-air-inhibited polyester finish or a catalyzed epoxy coating. Both finish types are toxic in the uncured state and require specialized finishing equipment not commonly available.

However, a relatively safe (and relatively expensive at about $60 a gallon) two-part, pour-on epoxy finish is available from Woodworkers Supply, Inc. (1108 North Glenn Rd., Casper, WY 82601; 800-645-9292). Maximum coating thicknesses of about 3⁄32 in. can be expected with this finish.

—CHRIS MINICK, *Stillwater, Minn.,*
from a question by Steve Petrosino, San Antonio, Tex.

Cracked Lacquer Finishes

SOME PERIOD-FURNITURE REPRODUCTIONS sport a "cracked" finish. The easiest way to mimic the cracked effect of an old shellac finish is with a special lacquer known as "crackle lacquer," available from most lacquer distributors. This finish handles just like regular lacquer, and is sprayed over a smooth coat of regular gloss lacquer to allow the crackle to occur properly. The size of the cracks in the finish is controlled by the heaviness of the sprayed coat—heavier coats yield bigger areas of cracking. A fine pattern of cracks can also be obtained by coating a sealed or partially finished surface with a mixture of white glue and gilder's whiting that's thinned considerably with water. When the film has dried, exposing it to a heat gun or blow dryer will cause cracking. This method is somewhat more controllable than using crackle lacquer, but the film is milky white instead of clear, so it is only effective with white or colored finishes. The glue/whiting mix can be colored with dry-powder pigments.

—MICHAEL DRESDNER, *Perkasie, Pa.,*
from a question by Ken Munsell, Litchfield, N.H.

Obtaining a Crackle Finish

THERE ARE AT LEAST TWO TECHNIQUES you can use to achieve a crackle finish that looks at least 100 years old—one that results in cracks in the top layer of paint and another that results in cracks in a clear coat over the top layer of paint. There are distinct aesthetic differences between the two techniques, so you may wish to experiment on sample boards before trying either technique on a finished product.

To crack the top layer of paint, you'll use a multistep process. You begin by applying a base coat of latex or milk paint to the bare wood. It should be a color that will contrast with the top coat. When this base coat is dry, apply a sealer coat of shellac. When the shellac is dry, scuff-sand, and then apply a coat of premixed liquid hide glue, such as Franklin's, over the shellac. Thinning the glue slightly with water will make the glue easier to brush. After waiting a few hours for the glue to dry thoroughly, apply a top coat of paint. As it dries, cracks will form, exposing the paint below. You can speed up the process with a hair dryer. When the paint is dry, apply a top coat such as shellac, varnish, or lacquer to protect the painted surface.

The second method, in which the clear top coat is cracked, uses two types of varnish, one over the other. It will work both as a clear finish and as a finish over a painted surface. First brush on a coat of oil-modified alkyd varnish. I use Pratt & Lambert clear #38, but many others will also work. Let this first coat dry until it's slightly tacky—usually about two hours.

You'll need to mix the second varnish because it's not commercially available. Dissolve one part gum-arabic powder (available from Chem-Lab Supplies; 714-630-7902) in two parts water. Heat this solution in a double boiler until all the gum arabic has dissolved, taking care not to let it come to a boil. Then remove it from the heat, and let it cool to room temperature. Add a few drops of dishwashing soap to help the solution flow more evenly, and brush it on over the tacky alkyd varnish. As the gum-arabic solution dries, it will crack. If cracks do not appear after several hours, a hair dryer set on warm will do the trick, but it's best not to force the process.

Wait a day for the gum arabic to dry fully; then accentuate the cracks by rubbing some artist's oil color into them, using a soft rag. I've used both Vandyke brown and burnt umber to good effect. Gum arabic is not very durable, so you'll want to apply a light top coat of shellac to protect the finish.

—JEFF JEWITT, *North Royalton, Ohio,*
from a question by Don Spittle, Beltsville, Md.

Making a New Paint Job Look Old

YOU CAN ARTIFICIALLY AGE PAINTS or lacquers in two ways. The first, sometimes used by manufacturers to produce novelty finishes, is called crackle lacquer. One extremely thick, wet coat of lacquer, either clear or tinted, is brushed on, allowed to air dry, then force-dried or baked in a 150°F oven for one to two hours (drying conditions vary from manufacturer to manufacturer). During force drying, the heat sets up stresses in the thick coat, causing wrinkles and a *craquelure* pattern. Since this process can't be closely controlled, the patterns formed can vary considerably.

The small valleys and cracks formed during the forced drying are accentuated by covering the entire surface with darker glazes (glazes for lacquer are available from Mohawk Finishing Products, Route 30 N., Amsterdam, NY 12010, and from Star Chemical Co., Inc., 360 Shore Dr., Hinsdale, IL 60521). When the glaze begins to set, wipe the bulk of it off, leaving the darker color only in the recesses and crackles. The colored glaze is then sealed in with a coat of clear lacquer.

The second way to age paint, lacquer, or another coating material, such as shellac, is more complicated and takes a more sophisticated touch. This method, which is closely akin to false graining, uses a colored ground coat, which is then covered with various layers of glaze applied by brush, rag, sponge, feather, airbrush, or spattering, depending on the texture you want. Glazes applied with crumpled paper, rag, or sponge produce a finish that resembles leather. Spatters are typically applied by running your thumb over a stiff toothbrush loaded with glaze, but go easy. There's nothing worse than a piece where someone went spatter-happy.

You can apply several colors of glazes, although apply them one at a time, and let each layer dry thoroughly before applying the next layer. While wet, each coat can be partially removed with rags, brushes, or feathers to simulate certain effects. Thin glazes on high points of an object show wear, for example, while thick coats indicate dirt accumulation. You can also simulate extra-heavy wear by sanding some areas down to the bare wood. Go easy and sand only those areas where the object would naturally be subject to heavy wear. All the glazes should be sealed with clear lacquer, shellac, or varnish. Usually, a sealer with a stain or flat sheen looks best.

—Robert D. Mussey Jr., *Waltham, Mass., from a question by E.S. Johnson, Rye, N.Y.*

Chapter 7

SPRAYING TIPS

Building a Home-Shop Spray Booth

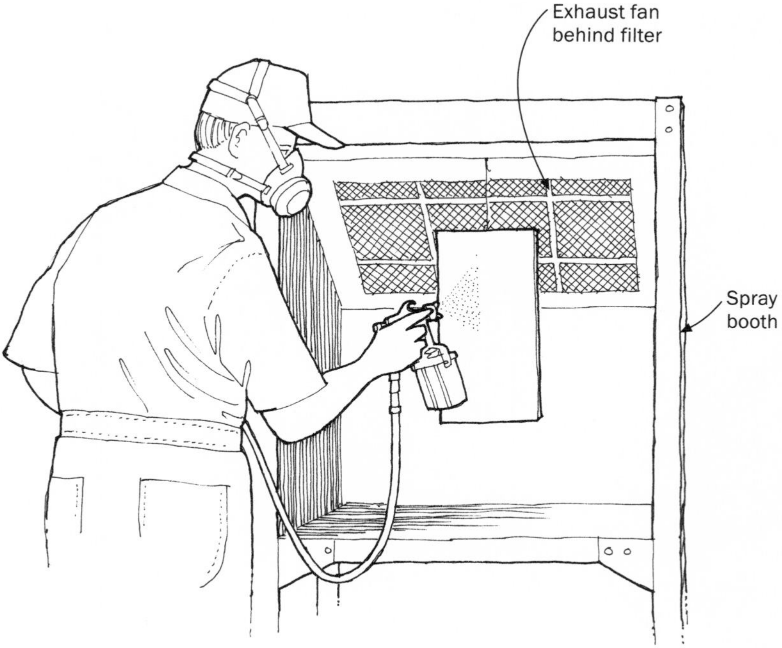

THE CRUCIAL ISSUE IN SETTING up a home-shop exhaust system is protecting against explosion and fire. At our professional woodworking shop, we bought a fan designed for spray booths from W. W. Grainger Inc. (5959 W. Howard St., Niles, IL 60648); the company offers several sizes and models. We use the tunnel-type fan with the nonsparking aluminum blades and the motor mounted outside the air stream.

In a home shop you should pick a fan large enough to change the air in your room fast enough to prevent fumes from collecting and creating an explosive atmosphere. But selecting a fan that's too big can rob your shop of heat and cause finishes to flash-dry on the surface. A common test for exhaust-fan effectiveness is to blow a puff of cigarette smoke in the room and, if all is well, the smoke will move steadily toward the fan. You should consult the manufacturers for fan-sizing information.

A good exhaust fan is, however, not enough to satisfy fire marshals and insurance inspectors. They are more concerned with lacquer buildup on the fan and the walls of the booth. The standard booth design, which you see in most cabinet, finishing, and auto-body shops, consists of three metal walls and a ceiling to form a booth as deep as the largest objects that are sprayed. A plenum with the fan at one end, attached to the back wall of the booth, draws the spray and fumes through a filter and out of the shop. Any electrical outlets, switches, or lights that could be the source of sparks must be outside the booth or, if they are inside, they must be special (and very expensive) explosion-proof. More typically, regular fluorescent lights are installed outside the booth, shining in through wire-glass windows.

Of course, the exhaust fan sucks in dusty air as quickly as it expels the fumes. Therefore, you must install some kind of filter between your spray booth or room and the outside. The idea is to filter the incoming air without creating too much air resistance for the exhaust fan, which will work it harder and wear out faster. Common furnace filters are not restrictive, so you won't have a problem with air resistance, but they aren't very effective dust removers either. A serious, cost-effective filter for your intake air is a dense-polyester type called Dicon, which is available from a local filter supplier. Allow plenty of filter surface so as not to restrict airflow.

Instead of buying the booth from a mail-order supplier or local dealer, we made ours using commercial steel studs and 22-gauge galvanized sheet metal. We put the whole thing together with self-taping screws, and ended up saving money and satisfying the inspectors. Many shops get by without having regulation booths, but then spray booth fires are all too common. Whatever you choose to do, make sure you use the proper-size exhaust fan, keep your booth free of lacquer buildup and overspray, and look out for sources of sparks. Particularly in the winter, when humidity is low, be careful of static electricity, which can also cause a fire.

As you can see, designing a spray booth involves a lot of compromises and judgment calls. Unfortunately, a well-engineered system is very expensive, but if you're a professional, it is a necessary, long-term investment.

—JOHN KRIEGSHAUSER, *Kansas City, Mo.,*
from a question by Dennis E. Hurley, Carlisle, Pa.

Spray-Booth Maintenance for Burning Eyes

IF, WHILE SPRAYING solvent-based finishes like nitrocellulose lacquer, you are wearing an organic vapor respirator but still have tired, burning, and red eyes and become a bit light-headed or disoriented, it is likely that your spray booth is not working as it should.

The first thing I'd do is replace the overspray arrestor filters. Chances are they're clogged, causing a decrease in airflow and subsequent buildup of vapors in the spray booth. While you're at it, vacuum out the chamber behind the filters, clean and lubricate the draft flapper doors, and check the blower-motor belt tension. If spray-booth maintenance doesn't alleviate the problem, then you need either a bigger spray booth or a full-face respirator. I find full-face respirators hot and uncomfortable, especially since I wear eyeglasses. A powered, air-purifying respirator (PAPR) may be a better alternative. PAPRs supply a constant stream of purified air to the face mask via a small, battery-powered air pump. Constant air pressure prevents solvents from entering the mask. PAPRs are not inexpensive. Expect to pay up to $500 for a good one. Personally, I would spend the money to upgrade the exhaust fan in my spray booth instead.

—CHRIS MINICK, *Stillwater, Minn.,*
from a question by David Otten, Chagrin Falls, Ohio

Clearing a Clouded Finish

IT'S A HOT, MUGGY DAY and you've just shot a heavy coat of lacquer on a nice project. A few minutes pass and you discover the finish has clouded with moisture. Here's how to clear the finish. Shoot the clouded area with acetone. The acetone will clear the finish and bring the moisture to the surface. Quickly wipe it off. To continue, thin the lacquer and shoot sparingly.

—ROBERT M. VAUGHAN, *Roanoke, Va.*

Window-Screen Holder for Spray-Finishing Small Items

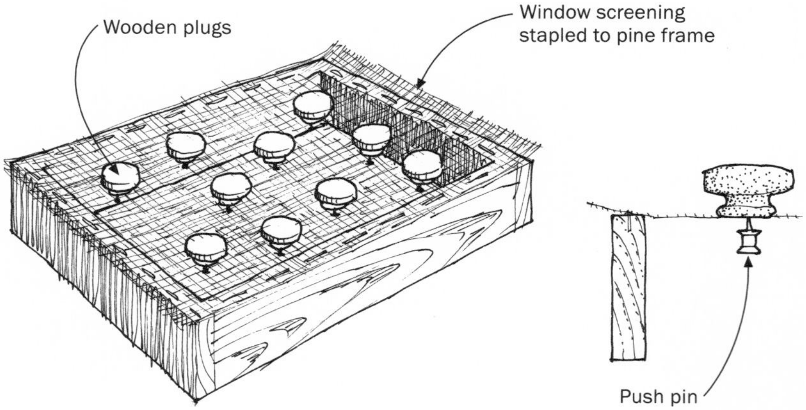

When I needed to finish a few dozen oak plugs for a new stair rail, I came up with a technique that solves most of the hassles of spray finishing small objects. I nailed together a scrap pine frame and stretched and stapled window screen across it. I then secured the plugs by inserting push pins through the screen into the bottom of each plug. Airflow through the screen eliminates sprayer blowback, which, in turn, eliminates blobs of paint or finish from forming on the bottoms of the plugs.

—James T. Jones Jr., *Fairfax, Va.*

Setup for Spray-Finishing Small Parts

When spraying small items, like the wooden marquetry jewelry that my wife, Lora, and I produce, it's difficult to get a fine spray finish without using so much air pressure that the pieces go flying. An efficient means of preventing this is simply to place them on a screen, so the air/lacquer overspray can continue through and not blow back. Plaster screen typically comes in 2-ft. by 4-ft. sections and is available at masonry supply houses or lumberyards. It makes a strong, inexpensive, and effective surface for those small items, and it can be cut to any convenient shape to suit your spraying purposes. Additionally, the twists in the expanded metal screen create tiny points that lift the object being sprayed, so they have little surface contact with the screen.

To facilitate spraying in my own small shop, I screwed a round piece of plywood to a lazy-Susan bearing and attached a piece of plaster screen to the plywood base with Sheetrock screws. Short (2-in.-long) sections of conduit were used as spacers between the screen and the base to lift the screen enough to allow the overspray to escape. I placed the lazy Susan atop a 24-in.-dia. plywood turntable powered by a 6-rpm fractional-horsepower motor (#22806, available from W. W. Grainger, 5959 W. Howard St., Niles, IL 60648; 312-647-8900). I can spin the lazy Susan by hand at any time, or I can switch on the turntable to automatically rotate the screen so that I can spray a lot of small items evenly.

To complete my inexpensive spray booth, I set the screen turntable in a corner of my shop and used an exhaust fan salvaged from a junked walk-in freezer to pull away the fumes and overspray. To speed drying, I mounted a squirrel-cage blower, fitted with an adjustable angling attachment (to vary airflow direction onto the object being sprayed), above the turntable. The fan and blower are wired to the same switch for convenience. I also clamped a flood lamp above the turntable, so I can see what I'm doing and check the evenness of the finish as I spray.

—SPIDER JOHNSON, *Mason, Tex., from a question by Les VanCleef, Lubbock, Tex.*

Safely Spraying Waterborne Finishes

MANY WOODWORKERS ARE considering changing over to waterborne finishes because they are designed to be safer for the environment than conventional solvent finishes. But this does not necessarily make these finishes safer to apply for the user. Waterborne finishes are alkaline mixtures (pH 8-8.5) of finishing polymers, solvent, various additives, and, of course, water. These finishes can irritate sensitive skin and damage the eyes if not handled correctly. And breathing difficulties may result from inhalation of the mists created during spraying operations. As you can see, waterborne finishes are far from benign.

The same safety precautions afforded solvent-based finishes must also be applied to waterborne finishes. You should wear protective eye goggles, a vapor respirator, and gloves when working with any finish regardless of the carrier solvent. Additional safety information can be obtained from the product Material Safety Data Sheet (request one from the manufacturer of your finish).

When spraying waterborne finishes, a spray booth is not just a luxury but is a vital piece of safety equipment. This is especially true if your spray equipment is the conventional high-pressured compressed-air type. High-pressure spray equipment in inexperienced hands can contaminate the entire area, including the user, with unwanted finish overspray. A good spray booth is necessary to contain this overspray. The decision to construct the spray booth with explosion-proof wiring and fire protection is really up to your local fire marshal and insurance carrier. Contact both of them for the pertinent regulations in your area. Be aware, though, a spray booth constructed to handle only waterborne finishes cannot be used for solvent-based finishes of any kind.

—CHRIS MINICK, *Stillwater, Minn.,*
from a question by Jeffrey H. Geisel, Orefield, Pa.

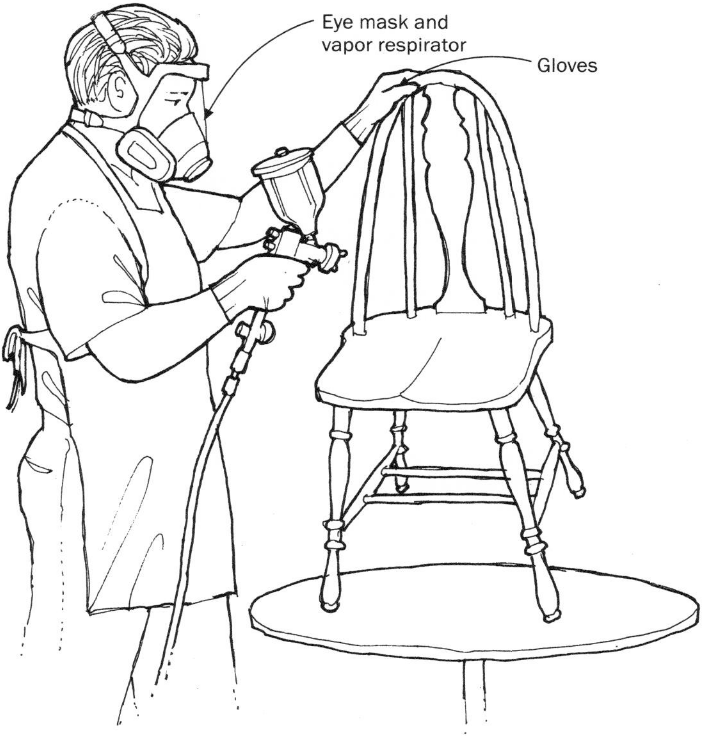

Designing a Finishing Room for Brushed-On Finishes

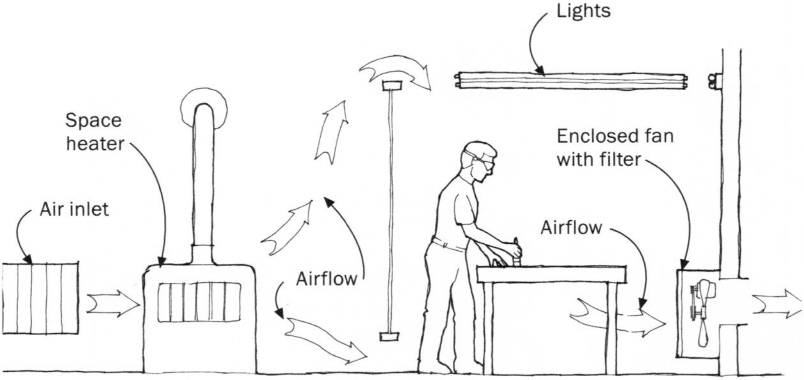

VENTILATION REQUIREMENTS for a finishing area where the finishing material will be wiped or brushed on rather than sprayed are quite different. Wiping or brushing is very efficient. Except for the occasional drip, all the material used is applied to the piece being finished, and there it sits till it dries or soaks in and the excess is removed with a rag. When spraying finish, only 60% to 85% of the finish material, depending on the efficiency of the equipment used, ever hits the project and sticks. The rest of the material is launched into the air in tiny droplets and quickly forms a noxious and explosive cloud. This cloud needs to be produced in a spark-free environment (for example, a spray booth) and exhausted to the outdoors through an explosion-proof fan.

The requirements for ventilating a non-spray finishing area are more like the requirements for a drying area. For this type of operation, you would not need a fireproof area. As long as you do not allow a buildup of drippings on the floor and practice common-sense housekeeping, there should be no conditions that are unusually dangerous. If your garage is unfinished inside, adding drywall will give it a nice finished surface, which would make the room easy to light and keep clean.

Your ventilation requirements are a fraction of what you would need during a spraying operation. I recommend a complete change of air in the area about every 10 to 15 minutes. For example, if you are finishing a dining table in the back of your garage and you drape some plastic sheeting to enclose an 8-ft. by 8-ft. area and your ceiling is 8 ft. high, you will need a fan that can move 51 cu. ft. per minute (cfm) to accomplish a complete air change in 10 minutes. The formula that's used to calculate fan size in this case is volume divided by time equals cmf. In the previous example:

8 ft. x 8 ft. x 8 ft. = 512 cu. ft.

512 cu. ft. / 10 min. = 51 cfm

Because vapors are heavier than air, I would mount the fan low on the outside wall, as shown in the drawing, with some kind of door on the outside that can be closed when not in use. Or use an inexpensive single-panel shutter that opens when the fan is turned on. If the fan is turned on at the onset of the finishing operation, you will have no buildup of fumes. Although you probably don't need an explosion-proof fan, you should check with your local fire marshal to be sure.

The heat required to make up what is lost to ventilation will be minimal with the drying room. Because the same amount of air that you exhaust will be drawn back in from cracks, doors, and windows all around the garage, I suggest you install a heat source in the garage but away from the vented area, to warm the air before it passes through the drying area. You could mount radiant heaters on the wall or use an electric baseboard in the area. I'd keep the heat source at least 3 ft. from the work.

Lighting can be fluorescent or incandescent and mounted so the bulbs are protected from being hit when working in the room. Light should reflect off the work at an angle, so you can see what you are doing. Place switches away from the area so they can be controlled without disturbing the work.

—THOMAS RICCI, *Lexington, Ky.,*
from a question by Richard A. Grimlund, North Liberty, Iowa

Lighting for a Finishing Room

MORE FINISH ON WOOD is ruined by improper lighting than by any other single cause. Yet few people worry about the light in the finishing room, and I've never seen any guidelines in books. So, here are my thoughts on the subject.

You must have as much light as you can possibly create, and it must be as close as possible to natural daylight. Your best bet are the 8-ft.-long fluorescent fixtures, with half the tubes cool white and half daylight-imitating. Install them as high as possible, well sheltered from dust, and clean them frequently.

Don't install the lights directly over the working area. The object you are working on should reflect the light to your eyes. Assume you are working on a flat object on top of your bench. If you put a flat mirror on top of your bench, you should be able to see the whole light fixture. The lower the angle of reflection, the better it is, the ideal being about 45°. This means that the angle between your eyes, the work, and the light should be about 90°.

I would go a step further and install one or two movable lights about 6 ft. off the floor, so you can arrange the light to reflect off the top of a high piece like a chair or chest.

Lights near the work or over the spraying area will have to be inside protective fixtures, and you might have to use incandescents. But all artificial lights distort colors—incandescents add a definite red hue. Never match colors by artificial light. Do it by daylight and in shadow.

—GEORGE FRANK, *South Venice, Fla., from a question by Eva Eshleman, Allentown, Pa.*

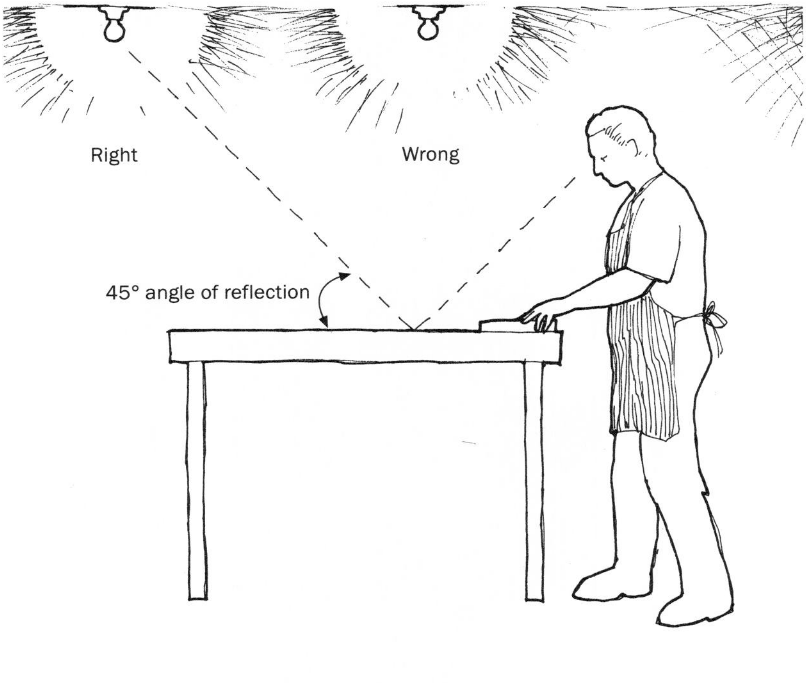

Plastic-Bag Paint-Pot Liners

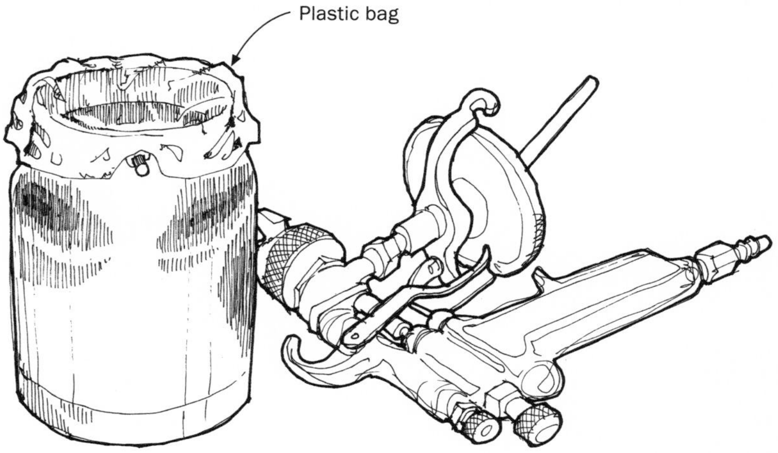

I KEEP A SUPPLY OF PLAIN one-gallon plastic food storage bags (without a zipperlike closure) to line the quart pot of my spray gun. This trick only works in pots with lever releases, not those that screw to the gun. I generally use two bags at a time, in case one should leak. The bags simplify waste disposal and minimize the amount of expensive solvent needed to clean the pot. I've never had any problem with solvents dissolving the bags.

If you're going to be spraying the leftover material soon, it may be sealed right in the bag with twist ties and stored in any empty quart paint can. However, if you leave paint sealed inside the bag for long, the material that dries on the inside of the bag may cause problems when spraying.

—BRUCE DE BENEDICTIS, *El Cerrito, Calif.*

Scraping out Runs

WHEN SPRAYING FURNITURE, runs are a fact of life, and trying to wipe them only makes a bigger mess. After years of spraying both lacquer and varnish, I finally discovered that you can let them dry and scrape them flush with a razor blade. Then recoat, or simply rub out the finish with pumice and oil.

—JON GULLET, *Washington, Ill.*

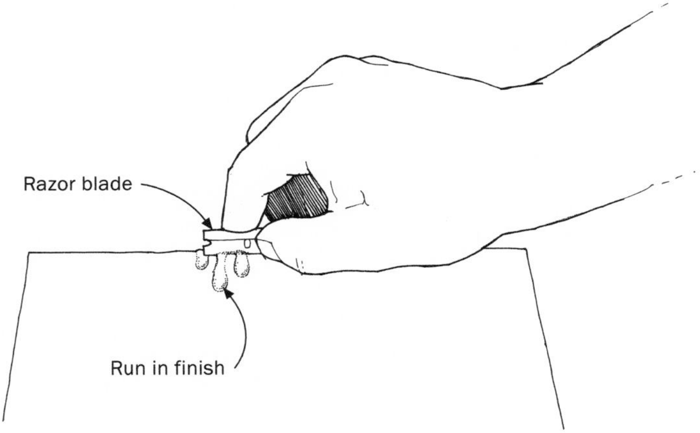

MINWAX
CLEAR SATIN
NET WT 11.5 OZ (326g)
ORIGINAL
FINISH
SPECIALTY PRODUCTS
ClearFlex UV
D308

Chapter 8

PREVENTING FADING

Finishing Bright-Colored Woods without Darkening

HERE'S AN OLD METHOD for finishing bright-colored woods, like vermilion, without darkening them. The answer lies not with the finish material, but with the tricky way of applying it. My choice would be fresh white shellac, but you can use picture varnish or water-white lacquer. The trick is to get the finishing material to contact the wood and dry at the same time, so the carrying agent (alcohol, thinner, or turpentine) has no time to enter the pores of the wood and darken it. I would use an air brush of the type commercial artists use (you can buy one for about $60 at an art-supply store) or a mouth sprayer. Regulate it to spray as much air and as little finish as possible, and hold it far from the work. The first coat must be infinitely light and thin. Succeeding applications can be a little heavier, but you must not rush. It will take a certain amount of skill and a great deal of patience. You could also try two coats of a dilute, lukewarm solution of bleached hide glue, well sanded under any clear finish.

—GEORGE FRANK, *South Venice, Fla., from a question by Kenneth Carl*

UV Absorber Slows Ultraviolet Deterioration

SPAR VARNISH USED AS AN EXTERIOR finish on redwood will, if exposed to direct sunlight, last less than a year before it begins to deteriorate from ultraviolet light. To slow the deterioration use a spar or super-spar varnish listing ultraviolet absorber on its label. UV rays will eventually destroy the film, though, no matter how durable it is. This, plus the expansion and contraction of the wood that weakens the film and permits it to crack, lets moisture creep in. Peeling and lifting result. To maintain a decent appearance don't build up a heavy surface film. Use two or three coats of well-thinned varnish, with drying time between, to get the film down into the wood.

You could also try an oil-based pigment stain such as wood-shingle coating. The pigment acts as a shield against UV light, and the oil base stays fairly flexible. But unless you use a lot of pigment, the redwood should be recoated every six to nine months. Clear marine epoxy varnish is sometimes mentioned for this purpose, but epoxy tends to chalk under ultraviolet. A better alternative would be Watco Redwood Finish and Waterlox Redwood Preserver, both in-surface finishes. Even with these you'll probably have to recoat in a year or so, but at least you won't have to sand off peeling surfaces.

—DON NEWELL, *Farmington, Mich., from a question by David McWethy, Fayetteville, Ark.*

Long-Lasting Clear Varnish for Exterior Applications

TO SLOW THE DETERIORATION of a clear exterior finish exposed to sunlight, try Awlgrip High Solids (U.S. Paint, Lacquer and Chemical, 2101 Singleton St., St. Louis, MO 63103). I have used this product on teak steering wheels for sailboats and also on mahogany and cedar dinghies with great success. I made a 26-in. teak wheel that has been out in the weather, including salt spray, for two years, and the finish is as bright as ever. Awlgrip is usually sprayed on over a sealer coat of varnish. I do not have a sprayer and find that a fine brush used carefully does just as well. I have also used this finish on a few of my recent pieces of furniture, ones that require a high gloss. It does not scratch easily and needs no attention except for the usual dusting.

—FREDERICK JOHNSON, *Andover, Mass.*

Avoiding UV Deterioration

RECENTLY I WAS SHOWN SOME OAK church doors which, although they had been carefully finished with several coats of good spar varnish, began to peel and flake off in less than a year. This is not that unusual. Spar varnish, marine varnish, and other similar exterior finishes almost always degrade within a year and require refinishing. The major cause is ultraviolet light, which attacks the molecular bonds in the varnish. Many current products contain UV-absorbing compounds, but they don't help all that much.

I suggest using a penetrating finish, which deposits protective materials inside the wood rather than building up on its surface. Penetrating finishes will also degrade in time, but since there's no surface film to worry about, refinishing is merely a matter of applying another coat or two of the same product. You may have to sand or steel-wool lightly to remove surface dirt before refinishing, but that's all the preparatory work required. In the case of the oak doors, since they had been varnished, you will have to remove this old finish and expose the bare wood before using a new penetrating finish.

Watco Exterior Wood Finish should serve well for this, or you might try Waterlox Marine Finish, thinned down a bit with mineral spirits to ensure good penetration. Brush on a first coat, keeping the surface fairly wet. When the wood has soaked up all the finish it will take, wipe it dry and let it harden overnight. Apply a second coat the next day, again wiping off the excess.

If you want to stay with surface film products, try ZAR Imperial Polyurethane or McCloskey Marine Varnish. Another preparation worth trying is called Deks Olje, put out by the Flood Co. (Hudson, OH 44236). It's a gloss finish for saltwater boat woodwork.

—DON NEWELL, *Farmington, Mich.,*
from a question by George Seibel, Stratford, Conn.

Keeping Padauk's Color

PADAUK STARTS OUT WITH BRILLIANT color when freshly cut, then darkens and turns brown with time. To shield the wood from ultraviolet light and thus effectively slow the darkening process, I use a product called Armor-All, a spray-on protective liquid for auto vinyl. This product, available at auto-supply stores, is quite effective—I have yet to see the color of padauk change, even after four years. To use, spray three or four coats of Armor-All on the wood before you apply the finish. I use an oil finish, which is compatible with Armor-All, but other finishes such as lacquer or varnish may not be. You'd best test the particular finish you plan to use.

—DAVID LEWIS, *Phoenix, Ariz.*

Keeping Purpleheart Purple

RECENTLY A FRIEND SHOWED ME a desk made of amaranth (purpleheart). The wood has a wax finish, and in four years has changed from a bright purple color to deep reddish-brown. He wanted to restore the desk to its original purple and preserve the color.

I explained that restoring the purpleheart color is easier than maintaining it, and he'll have a better chance of preserving it if he uses something other than a wax finish. If you're in the same situation, here is my advice. First, scrub the piece with turpentine, then rinse it with water to clean all the wax and other impurities off. You'll probably notice some of the purple color returning right away.

After letting the piece dry, sand it very lightly with 220-grit paper to remove the grain whiskers raised by the water. Sand gently in a circular or figure-eight motion, making sure every bit of the surface is covered. This type of sanding will remove all the raised grain (if you sanded only with the grain, you would push some of the grain back down, rather than cutting it off) and removes tiny amounts of surface material. Finish sanding with 320-grit or 400-grit sandpaper with the grain and you should be back to the original color.

There are numerous theories about how to maintain the color. The one thing that everyone agrees on is that light is at least partly responsible for the fading. This leads to a dilemma. You can hinder the passage of harmful ultraviolet rays in light with inhibitors (spar varnish is an example of a finish containing UV inhibitors), but you will be sacrificing the clarity and color of the wood by doing so. And why bother preserving the purple color if the finish makes it difficult to see it?

One alternative is to refinish the piece every five years or so. I'd recommend you use tung oil for resiliency and ease of application and removal. It will hold the color longer than plain wax. If you want to try a light-inhibiting finish, try spar varnish thinned 50/50 with paint thinner and tung oil. Another alternative is to cheat. Get a water-based aniline dye that matches the original color of the desk and apply it before finishing.

—DAVID SHAW, *Kelly Corners, N.Y.,*
from a question by Malcolm Fleming, Taos, N.M.

Finishing to Protect Wood's Color

OXIDATION AND LIGHT are probably the two biggest factors that cause wood to change color over time. This is especially true of some of the more brightly colored woods, including the exotics like padauk and rosewood, which are often highly susceptible to these influences. Just about any finish will slow the surface oxidation of wood, but overcoming the effects of light is a bit tougher.

It is generally thought that the ultraviolet range of the light spectrum is responsible for the lion's share of color fading. For that reason, finish manufacturers routinely add UV blockers or absorbers to exterior paints and varnishes. However, few manufacturers add them to interior coatings because these are intended for use under artificial lights, which do not put out such a heavy UV concentration. The obvious solution would be to simply choose a finish that contains UV blockers. Sadly, this isn't that easy to do in many cases, since few companies add UV blockers to interior lacquers and varnishes (and fewer still advertise the fact).

Some people suggest that Armor-All, a liquid designed to protect the vinyl on automotive interiors from UV degrade, will protect wood colors from fading as well. This is not surprising, since Armor-All contains UV blockers. Unfortunately, it also contains silicone. If it is applied to raw wood prior to coating, the silicone will contaminate the surface and cause fisheyes in most film-type finishes, such as lacquer or varnish. If Armor-All is applied over a dry, film-type finish, it will require reapplication every three to six months. On the other hand, it is not likely to create any problems under an oil finish.

Incidentally, if you find yourself having to remove Armor-All or silicone from a surface, Armor-All makes a "Car Cleaner" that contains a silicone surfactant that helps break silicone's normally tenacious hold on a surface.

—MICHAEL DRESDNER, *Perkasie, Pa.,*
from questions by Mike Hobgood, Tylertown, Miss.,
and Dan Quackenbush, Olathe, Kan.

Explaining the Color Change of Cocobolo

COCOBOLO IS A MEMBER of the rosewood genus, *Dalbergia*, and this genus produces some of the most brilliantly colored woods in the world. Often, however, these woods are not particularly vivid when first cut but tend to develop a richer, warmer color over time. For example, newly sawn cocobolo is an unattractive purplish-brown yellow whereas it turns a beautiful red-orange color after aging for a while.

The reason for this is that the wood contains organically produced volatile elements that oxidize upon exposure to the air. While these volatiles are not particularly complex in chemical structure initially, the oxygen in the air causes them to polymerize, forming more complex molecules, and, in turn, these polymers are often pigments. Many woods react to oxygen and other stimuli in the environment as they develop their unique patinas. For example, American black cherry, *Prunus serotina*, darkens when exposed to light, but light does not appear to be the only factor in creating the rich color cherry ultimately develops.

A wood's natural patina is the product of rather complicated chemical reactions, which are neither thoroughly understood nor easily controlled. Rubbing the freshly cut surface of some woods with one of several solvents, such as alcohol, acetone, or naphtha, will often cause an immediate change in the wood's color, but this interference in the natural process can lead to long-term disappointment. Rosewoods have such an outstanding potential for natural patina it is a shame to adulterate it. With this in mind, I recommend working the wood down to where all surfaces are the uniform color of the fresh wood, and then letting it develop its patina naturally. In only a few weeks, the wood will mellow enough in color to be very attractive, and it will go on to attain its full range of warm highlights, which it might never achieve if you attempt to hasten the process with harsh chemicals.

—JON ARNO, *Schaumburg, Ill., from a question by Charles Conyers, Toledo, Ohio*

Why Does Cherry Darken?

LIGHT IS THE PRIMARY FACTOR causing cherry to develop its renowned patina. When exposed to bright light, the wood will noticeably darken in a matter of hours, and it will continue to subtly change across the span of decades, if not centuries. I suspect exposure to the air, however, also plays a role. I've seen nothing in the literature that lends clarity to this complex subject, but by way of personal experience, I once stored some cherry lumber in a pitch-dark attic for several months and its color did in fact shift from flesh pink to amber brown. Why rough-sawn cherry darkens more slowly than the planed lumber is certainly consistent with its known photosensitivity: Loose wood fibers on the surface would tend to refract light. Although I haven't personally tried it (and it feels a bit excessive), a coat of opaque, nonporous paint might retard the wood's patina-forming process by providing a barrier to both light and air.

Some woodworkers are entirely too sensitive about cherry's tendency to blush, going so far as wrapping leftover milled stock in black plastic so it will match unmilled stock on the next project. Actually, this species' pronounced patina is one of its most attractive elements and helps make it the world-class cabinet wood that it is. There is no harm in combining pieces of cherry that are at slightly different points in their patina-building process. Sanding or remachining the cherry will usually lighten it somewhat, and once the project is complete, simply place it in bright light for a few days before applying the finish. It is far more important to avoid using sapwood when working with cherry because this immature wood tissue is, well, just too innocent to ever blush. And finally, don't use a UV-inhibiting varnish. The ultimate beauty of cherry rests in letting it do its thing.

—Jon Arno, *Troy, Mich., from a question by Robert Nanninga, Zeeland, Mich.*

Finish for Exterior Woodwork in Arid Climate

Woodwork exposed to strong ultraviolet light will require continuous maintenance. In the American Southwest, that means sanding away dried wood and oil and reoiling as often as four times a year. A varnished surface would require stripping, sanding, and revarnishing at least once, perhaps twice, a year.

An overhanging roof helps a lot. Yet in most cases, light from the rising and setting sun still reaches the woodwork. Clear, dry desert air deflects very little of the sun's most destructive rays. In New Mexico, we sometimes see a sort of "farmer's tan" on buildings where the upper portion of the woodwork, which never sees direct sunlight, remains relatively undamaged, and the lower portion of the woodwork looks barbecued.

So, for exterior woodwork in a sun-baked, arid climate, I'd recommend applying either paraffin dissolved in paint thinner or hot oil. A lamb's wool paint roller works well. Neither finish will last as long or protect as well as varnish, but they're easier to maintain and look far better between maintenance coats.

You can formulate your own finish with linseed oil, paraffin, and paint thinner. Adding Japan drier will cause the mix to cure rather than just dry. Use a flameless heater away from your beautiful new building to warm and dissolve the paraffin, but don't overheat it.

Apply the mixture continuously until the surface remains wet. Let it soak in until glossiness begins to disappear, and then wipe it down. Repeat daily until you find the balance point between filling the pores and too much surface buildup.

—Sven Hanson, *Albuquerque, N.M.,*
from a question by Yoram Tencer, Eilot, Israel

Need a Good Sunscreen?

RECENTLY I WAS ASKED TO RECOMMEND a polyurethane finish that will inhibit the darkening of wood caused by light degradation. Actually, ultraviolet light is only one of the many factors that contribute to the darkening of wood. Moisture, heat, visible light, and time also take their toll. UV absorbers may marginally slow the wood darkening phenomena, but they are, in a manner of speaking, sacrificial lambs. Depending on molecular structure, UV absorbers either directly absorb UV radiation and dissipate it as harmless heat or absorb the free radicals generated when UV radiation strikes a finish molecule. In any case, the absorber molecules are eventually consumed and unable to protect anything. Some UV absorbers actually accelerate the yellowing of the finish film as they are consumed (they are designed to maintain film integrity, not film color).

UV absorbers are great for finishes used indoors. Common double-glazed window glass screens out about 85% of the naturally occurring UV radiation, so little of it reaches inside the house anyway.

UV absorbers aside, a polyurethane furniture finish is not the best choice for minimizing discoloration. A better choice would be an acrylic-based furniture finish. Acrylic finishes resist UV degradation, have good protective properties, are exceptionally clear, and remain that way for the life of the finish.

Age darkening of wood is inevitable. My advice is to apply a good acrylic finish, and let your heirloom age gracefully.

—CHRIS MINICK, *Stillwater, Minn.,*
from a question by Will Gleim, Willingboro, N.J.

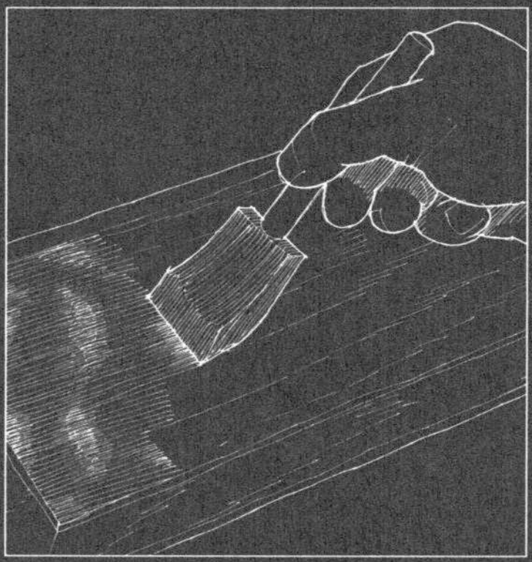

Chapter 9

TROUBLESHOOTING FINISHING PROBLEMS

Problems with a Bleeding Danish Oil Finish

WITH A DANISH OIL FINISH, care must be taken to avoid oil bleeding from the finish and to make sure the finish is as protective as it can be. For example, you're applying a Danish oil finish to a red-oak kitchen bar top. After sanding it down to 220-grit, you applied the oil in accordance with the directions on the can. However, you had a hard time getting the surface dry without more oil bleeding out of the pores and had to continue wiping down the top for two days. Once the finish finally dried, you waited a few days and then waxed it. However, the top doesn't seem to be very durable or resistant to stains.

These problems stem from some basic misunderstanding concerning Danish oil finishes, most of which are quite similar. These finishes are actually extremely thin, long oil varnishes, consisting of linseed oil cut with a large amount of mineral spirits and buffered with a small amount of alkyd resin. After the mineral spirits evaporate, the oil makes a poor moisture barrier. The bulk of the protection comes from the resin, but there is little of that in many mixtures I've used.

The problem with oil bleeding during application was a result of overloading the oak's especially large pores with this mixture of mineral spirits and oil, and this made it virtually impossible for the finish to dry. And you ended up probably wiping off the lion's share of finish you had applied, leaving little, if any, protective coating. Even under the best circumstances, one coat of Danish oil is a poor barrier for moisture resistance or heavy wear. And waxing the surface will do little to help; although wax, when applied over a finish, will repel water, it is a poor moisture barrier.

Next time, put on at least three or four lighter coats of Danish oil, allowing the film to completely dry between coats. Or better still, switch to a more protective varnish or polyurethane finish. Asking a single coat of Danish oil to stand up to the daily rigors of a bar top just isn't realistic.

—MICHAEL DRESDNER, *Perkasie, Pa.,*
from a question by Dennis E. Hurley, Carlisle, Pa.

Oil Bleeding Problems with Clear Watco Oil

YOU'VE OILED SEVERAL RAISED-PANEL mahogany doors with clear Watco oil. After the oil dried overnight, there was a thick sludge of oil that couldn't be removed from the surface. The manufacturer's instructions say to reoil and wipe immediately, but this didn't help. You called Watco and was told the oil works its way out of the pores and that lacquer thinner will clean it up. What should you do now?

Varnishes and sealing oils, such as linseed, tung, and Watco Danish oil, cure and harden through a process of solvent release and polymerization. As the turpentine, mineral spirits, or other solvents evaporate, the resin molecules link up and form a hard film that can no longer be dissolved by these solvents. When you spread one of the oils onto a porous wood, such as oak, walnut, or mahogany, the oil penetrates fairly deeply into the pores and remains there even after the surface excess is wiped off. Even though the oil immediately begins to polymerize over any surface exposed to air, the resins will have trouble linking up over the pores because the solvents continue to break through as they evaporate. As the solvents come to the surface, they carry along resins that spread out around the pores. If these resins are not wiped off in time, they polymerize on the surface, forming hard shiny spots, much like scabs over wounds. The problem is worse on warm days or when the wood is moved to a warmer atmosphere, which excites the molecules of the trapped solvents. It can occur even on cold days, though.

I don't know of any way to stop oil from bleeding, but I have found that I can avoid the problem if I apply the oil early in the day and wipe the surface every hour or two before the resins have a chance to harden. The bleeding usually stops by the end of the day. The next coat causes fewer problems because the pores are now partially or fully sealed. Neither the application of more oil nor lacquer thinner will remove fully cured spots. These spots should be abraded off with fine steel wool or sandpaper, possibly using some more oil as a lubricant. As a last resort, the finish should be removed with paint and varnish remover, and you should start over.

—BOB FLEXNER, *Norman, Okla.,*
from a question by Tim Tomaselli, Salt Point, N.Y.

Rosewood Won't Take Oil Finish

SOMETIMES AN OIL FINISH is just not the right choice for certain woods. As an example, you've built a dining-room table from South American rosewood and applied an oil finish made of ⅓ pure tung oil, ⅓ linseed oil, and ⅓ semigloss polyurethane. Some of the wood is kiln-dried, some is air-dried. The problem is that while the kiln-dried wood takes the oil beautifully, the streaks in the air-dried wood will not accept the finish.

All the genuine rosewood species (*Dalbergia*) contain varying amounts of natural resins and oils. These resins can react with the solvents present in many oil-based finishes, and as a result, oil-based finishes often will not dry or cure when applied to rosewood. It's most likely that the kiln-dried wood used is a rosewood substitute, like morado (*Machearium scleroxylon*, often marketed as Bolivian or Santos rosewood). This would explain why it took the oil finish without problems, while the heavily streaked wood did not.

Another source for problems might be the oil mixture. As a rule, it's not wise to mix finishes that are not intended to be mixed. You may get lucky every now and then, but more than likely you will create a nightmare like the one described here. Pure oils like 100% tung oil or boiled linseed oil might work on rosewood by themselves, but I doubt they're compatible with polyurethane. If you feel absolutely compelled to mix your own finishes, by all means check with a chemist or technical consultant at the company that makes the products you're using. Also, always do a test on a scrap or on the underside of your piece before applying your new concoction.

To finish the table, I'd skip oils altogether. If you are after the appearance of a hand-rubbed oil finish, you can achieve it with vinyl sealer and nitrocellulose lacquer and avoid all the problems of oil finishes. First, use a paint remover containing methylene chloride to remove the mess that the other finish left on your tabletop (the remover breaks the bonds that the polymerized oils in the finish have formed). Next, sand the rosewood with 200-grit sandpaper, and don't wait more than 10 minutes before you apply the new finish. Spray a coat of vinyl sealer light enough to leave the wood pores open. After the vinyl has dried, scuff the surface lightly with Scotch-Brite pads to deburr the raised grain. Then, spray two light coats of either flat, matte, or satin nitrocellulose lacquer in rapid succession. Wait a day, rub out the finish with 0000 steel wool to remove the sheen, and finish with paste wax.

—Dick Boak, *Nazareth, Pa.,*
from a question by Larry L. Brooks, Battle Ground, Wash.

White Dots in a Mahogany Finish

SIX MONTHS AGO, you finished a mahogany dining-room table with a high-gloss lacquer. After applying a paste wood filler, you let the table dry for days before sealing it. The buffed-out surface looked perfect. Several months later, random patches of white appeared in the finish, as if it has blushed. In addition, there were countless tiny white dots at the base of the finish, down at the wood level. What happened?

Apparently, oil from the filler mixture was absorbed into the pores of the mahogany, held there, and later released back into the filler after the finish had dried. The oil reacting with the filler forms a tiny white dot at the mouth of each pore. For some reason, this only occurs in mahogany, not walnut or any other wood with similar pores; even then, it happens only occasionally.

Unfortunately, there is no way to remove the dots, short of refinishing. My suggestion for avoiding it in the future is to lightly seal the mahogany before filling thus preventing excess oil absorption. This is done by applying one very thin coat of vinyl sealer on the wood prior to filling but after it has been stained. (This vinyl sealer is available at professional paint stores. Don't use regular lacquer sanding sealer.) Applying the vinyl sealer will also make the excess filler a bit easier to remove, and if the filler is pigmented, will prevent it from coloring any of the wood except for the pores themselves. After the filler has been wiped off, left to dry, and lightly scuffed to remove any surface residue, the piece can be resealed with another coat of vinyl before moving on to the lacquer top coats. In this way, you have essentially created a vinyl "envelope" that isolates the pocket of filler in each pore from the mahogany itself.

—MICHAEL DRESDNER, *Perkasie, Pa.,*
from a question by Phil Hostetter, New York, N.Y.

Slow-Drying Tung Oil

OIL FINISHES ARE POPULAR with woodworkers because they are easy to apply, give consistent, predictable results, and are easy to repair. They do have two major drawbacks though: long drying times and marginal protection qualities.

You've purchased a can of pure tung oil and applied a thick coat according to the directions on the can. The finish was extremely slow to dry. There are two reasons for this: First, all vegetable oils, such as tung oil, contain naturally occurring antioxidants that prevent the oil from hardening while still in the plant. These antioxidants must evaporate from the oil before any drying can take place. Hence, applying a too-thick coat of oil will retard the release of the antioxidants, resulting in a long drying time.

Second, oils dry by a process called oxidative polymerization. Oxygen is absorbed from the air and causes the oil molecules to crosslink, forming the finish film. As you would expect, the surface of a heavy coat of oil dries first, skins over, and forms an effective oxygen barrier. Oxygen must now diffuse through the cured surface film to polymerize the oil that's uncured below, which is a very slow process. Metallic driers can be added to most drying oils to speed up the drying process. This fix doesn't work with all oils though, tung oil being the most famous exception. Tung oil polymerizes by a unique mechanism and will not respond to metallic drier treatment.

Two things can be done to overcome the drying problems. If you prefer to use conventional oil finishes, such as raw tung or linseed, apply very thin coats and wait at least 24 hours between coats. The better solution, though, is to use a modified drying oil, like polymerized tung oil or one of the Danish oil products. Regardless of brand, traditional Danish oil finishes are mixtures of alkyd resins, drying oils, and solvents. These products look, act, and apply like conventional oils but eliminate the lengthy drying time. This added benefit provided by the alkyd modification provides a harder, more durable finish that still retains the easy repairability feature of conventional oils.

As with conventional oils, the key to success when using any drying oil as a finish is to apply multiple thin coats. Eight to ten coats may be necessary to provide sufficient protection for heavily used furniture, such as dining-room tables. A sufficiently thin coat can be applied by using a wipe-on/wipe-off technique. Saturate a cloth with oil and wipe a liberal coat on your project. Apply enough oil to visually wet the surface. Then allow the oil to soak into the wood for 20 to 30 minutes and wipe off the excess. Let the remaining thin oil film dry for at least 24 hours, and repeat the process until you are satisfied with the appearance.

—CHRIS MINICK, *Stillwater, Minn.,*
from a question by Antony Porter, Lorpoint, Cornwall, England

Hazy Oil Finish

HERE'S ANOTHER POSSIBLE PROBLEM: You built a bookcase of padauk and finished it with natural Watco Danish oil finish. After eight months you noticed a white haze forming on the surfaces of both the shelves and the uprights. The haze is easily removed by wiping with a dry rag. Is there anything you can do to prevent this haze?

A white haze forming on the surface of the oil finish is not normal. It could be a case of "blooming," which is the migration of some component of the finish to the surface where it interferes with the reflectance of light. I have not seen any problems from oil finishes on padauk with any of the brand-name formulations, so I think this is an anomaly. Although it may be difficult to say what is causing the haze, here are some simple procedures to find a solution.

First put a question mark with a permanent marker on the can of Watco, and use it up on odd jobs, not on anything special. Accept the idea that it's hard to track down the cause of the problem either in the can or in the application environment. When using this oil, proceed in small steps, making sure the surface is clean, dry, and smooth before putting on any oil. This should take care of most problems without creating new ones.

Next, pick a shelf not easily seen in day-to-day use, and test it in this manner. Wash the shelf with naphtha and a clean cloth, and let it dry. Sand it lightly as you did between coats of the original finish. Remove the dust from the surface, and apply a coat from a fresh can of Watco. Be sure to shake it up well, and follow the directions on the can. Let it dry, and see if the hazing returns in the following months. By sticking to the same formulation, the appearance of the finish is not changed as it might be if you switched to another brand with a different clarity or sheen.

Finally, when you are satisfied with the sample shelf, continue to clean and recoat the rest of the bookcase. The finish might have been contaminated in some way that prevented it from drying thoroughly. The driers in the additional coat could promote further curing or seal in the problem. Should this prove unsatisfactory, the next step would be to refinish the bookcase.

—NANCY LINDQUIST, *Chicago, Ill., from a question by Ernest L. Umbrico, St. Catharines, Ont., Canada*

Finishing Method for Teak

YOU FINISH A PIECE OF TEAK furniture with an oil finish that turns the wood reddish brown. You would prefer the look of commercial teak furniture that appears more yellow and has more surface gloss, which you don't have with the oil finish. How can you finish your piece to resemble the more common teak finish?

Commercial manufacturers are unlikely to reveal any of their trade secrets for finishes, but here's a method that should help you achieve the effect they achieve. Teak has a bad reputation with many finishers because it contains an oil that comes to the surface, thereby interfering with the adhesion of any film-forming coating. As a result, coatings like varnish or lacquer tend to peel off in six months to a year.

To avoid this peeling, I'd recommend washing the teak with a mixture of 90% alcohol by volume and 10% commercial-grade phosphoric acid. Be careful and wear rubber gloves to prevent skin contact. Apply the solution freely. Don't just dampen the teak. After the wood dries, repeat the alcohol treatment and let the wood dry again. Then apply a clear vinyl sealer (available from Sherwin Williams Co., 101 Prospect Ave., Cleveland, OH 44115, and its local distributors) followed by several coats of lacquer or varnish.

—OTTO HEUER, *Waukegan, Ill., from a question by Kenneth J. Rerie, Man., Canada*

Bubbles in a Spar Varnish Finish

CHANGES IN THE MANUFACTURE of finish products can result in unexpected problems. You've finished some exterior mahogany paneling by brushing on several coats of commercial spar varnish. You worked during a warm, dry week, waited 24 hours, and sanded between coats. However, the final coats developed air bubbles that dried in the varnish. Why did this happen?

Here's one possible answer. Recent government legislation requires finish manufacturers to reduce solvent levels in their products. To comply, some makers have increased the resin content in their mixtures, resulting in higher-solids finishes that go on thicker per application. While a thicker film is usually beneficial with most varnishes, this is not so with spar varnish, which customarily contains tung-oil-modified phenolic resins, making the varnish bubble and wrinkle when applied in a thick film. Unfortunately, this tendency is inherent in the drying process and can't be controlled by the user. To ensure better success in the future, apply spar varnish sparingly, brushing out or spraying on each coat as thinly as possible. Also, notify the manufacturer of your dissatisfaction with the product. Reputable manufacturers are sensitive to customer problems and many will compensate you for your inconvenience.

—CHRIS MINICK, *Stillwater, Minn.,*
from a question by Ken Jacobs, Waxahachie, Tex.

Dealing with Specks in a Finish

FINISHING TO A HIGH GLOSS can be difficult. Your goal may be to produce a finish with a high gloss that is perfectly smooth to both sight and touch. But you find that you always have to rub down your final finish to get rid of small specks in the surface, whether you've used varnish, lacquer, or enamel paint. Having to do this as a last step is a lot of work, and though you can restore a satiny gloss to a piece, you can never get back the original high gloss.

These nibs and specks in a brushed-on finish usually can be traced to one of three sources—bubbles in the finish, a dirty brush, or dust in the shop.

Thinning the finish combined with the proper brush technique will eliminate most bubble problems. I've found most brush-on finishes are too thick right from the can, so I thin my brushing finishes to the consistency of whole milk before application (about 13 seconds with a Zahn #3 viscosity cup).

Proper brush technique is important, too. A slip-slap back and forth stroke is okay for house painting, but it can be disastrous on fine furniture. Instead, flow the finish onto your project with long, even strokes similar to the techniques used for shellac.

A surprising number of specks in the finish film can be traced to a dirty brush. When a brush is used to apply finish, a small amount of finish works its way up the bristles and accumulates just below the ferrule. This area of the brush is difficult to clean completely, so the likelihood of residual dried finish in this area is high.

The next time the brush is used, dry finish flakes off and falls onto the wet finish film. Wetting your brush with thinner before sticking it into the finish will minimize this problem. Incidentally, new brushes often contain all sorts of junk and should be thoroughly cleaned before use.

Dust can be a real problem for woodworkers, like me, who don't have a separate finishing room. I've found the best time to do my finishing is late at night. I vacuum and blow down the shop and then eat supper. After two hours or so, I go back to the shop and start finishing. This quiet time allows the airborne dust to settle and cuts down on the specking problem.

I have a makeshift room for finishing (more of a tent than a room) made from heavy plastic sheeting. The plastic sheeting runs from the floor to the ceiling and makes a booth about 6 ft. square. This area keeps the dust and bugs out of my finish and doesn't work too badly as a spray booth for waterborne finishes, either. I use a 20-in. fan for ventilation when I spray. The excess air escapes through a false wall at the back of the booth. When I'm not using it, I roll up the finishing booth and store it against the ceiling with elastic cords.

If I were a betting man, I'd wager that most of those smooth high-gloss finishes you see have been rubbed out. Rubbing out, or "finishing the finish," is a necessary part of high-quality furniture finishing and should not be viewed as just an extra step to get rid of the specks. Specks and nibs are a part of finishing. We all get them, and we all have to rub them out.

—Chris Minick, *Stillwater, Minn.,*
from a question by Jack Hall, Newport Beach, Calif.

Blushing Lacquer

WHEN SPRAYING LACQUER in high humidity, blushing can be a problem. A mist coat with a large percentage of thinner might blush, while a coat of unthinned lacquer doesn't. Spraying a guitar body, you can often see the pattern of the internal bracing when blushing occurs; the braces seem to inhibit blushing, which occurs everywhere else on the thin soundboard and back.

Lacquer blushes when atmospheric water vapor condenses on the newly sprayed surface. When lacquer is sprayed, the sudden release of compressed air and the extremely high evaporation rate of the lacquer thinner combine to super-cool the surface, inviting condensation. The more thinner in the finish, the more cooling, which explains why the unthinned lacquer doesn't blush. The internal bracing in a guitar body acts as a heat sink, warming the lacquer and reducing the blushing effect directly over the brace.

To avoid blushing, avoid spraying on especially humid days. If you must, use a retarder to slow the evaporation rate. When blushing does occur, allow the lacquer to dry at least an hour, then wipe with 0000 steel wool.

—GEORGE MORRIS, *Post Mills, Vt.,*
from a question by Abraham Wechter, Pau Pau, Mich.

Avoiding a Chalky Finish when French Polishing

When French polishing you can get lovely results initially. Over time, however, the pores of the grain may look chalky, as if moisture were trapped.

French polishing imparts depth and luster to wood that is usually only obtained with thick application of varnish or lacquer. The reason that such depth and clarity can be achieved with such a thin application of shellac has to do with the substance used to fill the pores—pumice. Pumice is also the culprit in most problems with French polishing.

In traditional French polishing, 4F pumice is used to fill the pores of open-pored woods like mahogany and oak, but it can also be used on small-pored woods like cherry. The pumice is sprinkled onto the surface with a pad called a tampon that has an inner core charged with a little shellac and alcohol. The idea is that the pad abrades the surface of the wood with the pumice and makes a "paste" of oil, wood dust, shellac, and pumice that serves as a very transparent pore filler. This is where problems can arise.

Pumice is a white powder and is very high in silica content. Because it is essentially powdered glass, it has a low refractive index. In mediums such as oils or shellac, pumice becomes transparent when these products surround the irregular microscopic glass fragments. This works fine as long as the medium dispersed around the pumice particle is invisible. But when the pumice is no longer dispersed by shellac or oil, it will revert back to its white appearance and cause a chalky or cloudy effect under the finish. There are two ways to overcome this problem during application. The first method involves an adjustment in technique. After oiling the wood (I prefer linseed oil), sprinkle pumice on the surface. Then saturate some padding cloth with a 2-lb. cut shellac solution so that it's practically dripping wet. Using this shellac-soaked rag, wipe the pumice into the wood with circular motions and frequently recharge the pad with shellac. This technique assures that the pumice is mixed with plenty of shellac to keep it transparent.

The other method you can use is simply to premix the pumice and shellac and then apply this "filler" almost like a paste wood filler. To make the filler, dissolve 4 oz. (by weight) of shellac flakes into 4 oz. (by volume) of denatured alcohol. After the flakes have dissolved, stir in 3 oz. to 4 oz. (by volume) of 4F pumice. Stir thoroughly and then apply this thick mixture with a stiff-bristle brush to the surface you're polishing. Scrape the excess off with a rubber squeegee and then remove the excess with an alcohol-dampened cloth. After drying, any excess can be sanded off. This technique is tricky on larger surfaces, but it's perfect for complex surfaces where it's hard to work the pumice into corners.

To solve the chalkiness problem, you have to work shellac in the pumice that's trapped in the surface and pores of the wood. Saturate the surface with alcohol to dissolve the shellac on the surface and then scrub with a gray abrasive pad. Periodically squirt some 2-lb. cut shellac on the surface to mix into the slurry you'll kick up. This should work into the pumice and disperse it enough to make it transparent again.

—JEFF JEWITT, *North Royalton, Ohio,*
from a question by Cynthia Neer, Boston, Mass.

Curing Lacquer Orange Peel

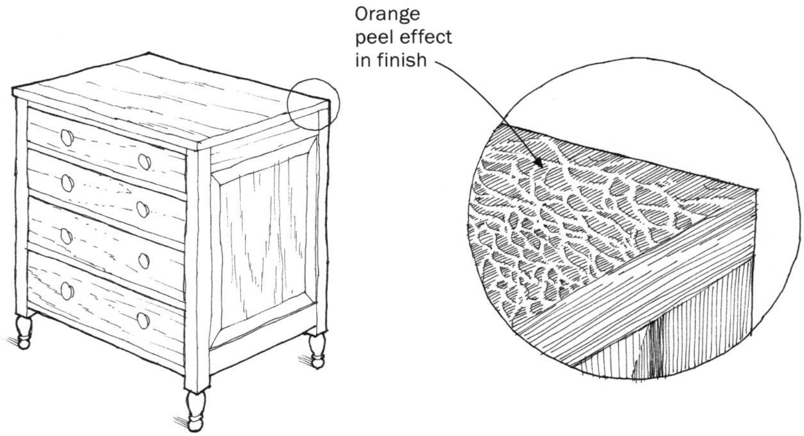

ONE POSSIBLE PROBLEM WITH sprayed lacquer finishes is orange peel—a crinkling disfigurement of the lacquer film as it dries. Various solutions you might try include thinning the lacquer, changing nozzles on the spray gun, and moving the gun more slowly during spraying.

If none of these work, you must realize that orange peel is caused by the lacquer drying or turning to gel on the surface it is sprayed on before it has a chance to flow and level. If thinning the lacquer doesn't help, try raising the temperature of your spray area or of the surface being sprayed. Spraying conditions that are too cool cause the lacquer to gel before it can flow and level itself—it then dries in a rough, orange-peel surface. Heating the lacquer slightly may also help, but use only a non-flame heat source. I usually put the lacquer cup in front of a heat register for a few minutes before spraying. If the air pressure to the spray gun is too low, the lacquer will not atomize properly, resulting in the poor flow and leveling that cause orange peel. Airless-type spray guns can be particularly troublesome in this regard. Holding the gun at just the right distance from the surface is also important, and you should move it just steadily enough to apply as much lacquer as possible without causing drips and runs. If nothing else seems to work, lacquer manufacturers make additives that can be mixed into their finishes to retard orange peel. Finally, you can correct an orange peel surface by wet-sanding back to the previous coat and respraying the surface with fresh lacquer.

—GEORGE MORRIS, *Post Mills, Vt.,*
from a question by Michel Chevanelle, Acton Vale, Que., Canada

Cratered Finish

HERE'S A REAL NIGHTMARE in refinishing a tabletop. You removed the original finish with Hope's Furniture Refinisher and then applied a polyurethane finish, but it cratered in small spots. You then removed the polyurethane finish with Formby's Paint Remover, sanded the top down to bare wood, and re-stained it. Next you applied Deft. This finish also cratered. What's causing this?

At some time, silicone must have been applied to the tabletop—perhaps in a polish. Silicone is very tenacious stuff, and solvents and removers tend to spread it around rather than remove it. These craters, called "fisheyes," happen when silicone prevents the finish from adhering.

Wet 400-grit wet-or-dry sandpaper with mineral spirits, and sand down to bare wood. Dry the wood and wipe off all the sanding dust. If you're going to re-stain, do it now. Next, brush on a very thin coat of shellac, thinned three parts denatured alcohol to one part shellac. Don't build up a thick layer. Let this dry, and apply Deft normally. You should not have cratering this time. To be absolutely sure, I'd add a small amount of fisheye flowout (available from Woodworker's Supply, 1108 N. Glenn Rd., Casper, WY 82601; 800-645-9292) to the Deft; it's an additive designed to eliminate fisheyes caused by silicone and other impurities.

—DON NEWELL, *Farmington, Mich.,*
from a question by R. William Furman, Ft. Collins, Colo.

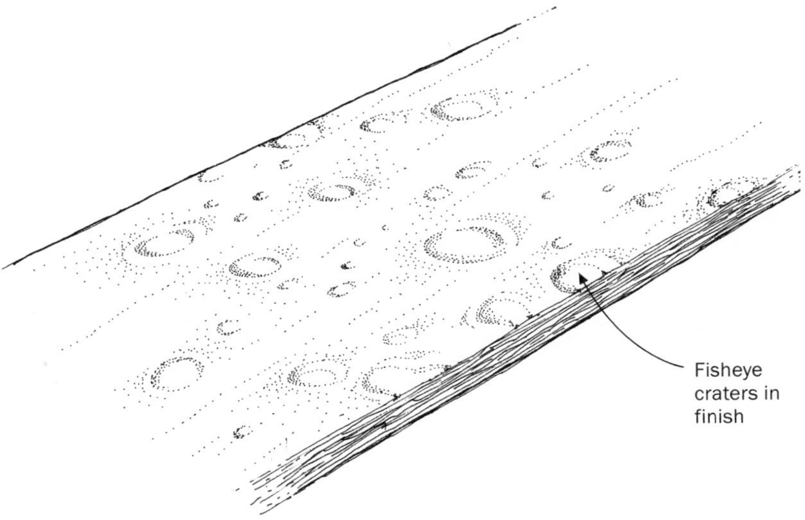

Eliminating Fisheyes in Varnish Finish

IF THE VARNISH ON YOUR REFINISHED TABLE cratered and peeled off, this problem is known in the trade as fisheyes. Its cause is residue either from waxes and silicone polishes such as Pledge, or from stripping chemicals. Always wash the wood with alcohol after stripping. Cratering is common in auto body repairing, and auto-supply houses sell various brands of a product called fisheye eliminator. It should be mixed with lacquer, enamel, varnish, or sealer before applying each coat.

—FINE WOODWORKING EDITORS, *from a question by James Smith*

Repelling Lacquer

YOU ARE HAVING A PROBLEM with lacquer repelling, or forming fisheyes, on several refinished pieces of furniture. The pieces were the type that can be found in any national furniture store. Much of the wood in the furniture seems to have been darkened with a substance that appears black in the grain. You sanded all of the pieces way beyond what would be normal, but the black still remains. You wiped the pieces with silicone wash and then stained, sealed, and shot them with lacquer. You ended up with fisheyes as large as ¼ in. over all the areas that had the black stain. The only solution you could find was to stain, glaze, and then spray on a very light dust coat of lacquer. While the fisheye has been eliminated, the finish is far from satisfactory.

These fisheyes may have been caused by traces of a penetrating oil stain used on the lighter parts of the wood to make them match the darker parts. Such stain can sometimes bleed through the finish coat and cause problems. This would be my assumption because the precaution of a silicone wash was taken, the wood was sealed well prior to top-coating it, and the fisheyes occurred only on the black-stained areas.

The volatile nature of lacquer increases the likelihood of this happening. I suggest that you isolate your stained surface with a thinned-out wash coat of dewaxed white shellac, and then proceed with the finish of your choice. Though shellac is not ordinarily used under lacquer finishes, it is compatible if you mist a coat of sanding sealer over it. It does a superb job of sealing stained surfaces so that subsequent finishes can be applied without too many problems. You can buy shellac in spray cans, which is very convenient for such jobs.

I would caution that not all commercially available stains are compatible with all top coats. I've had problems with various finishes, including polyurethanes, developing fisheyes when used over certain stains. You should experiment with different combinations of stain/top coat systems to achieve professional results. Don't assume all major name-brand products will work in all situations. Which type of stain will give you the least amount of trouble in terms of applying a top coat? I believe water-soluble aniline dye, which is dissolved in water, would be the least reactive with lacquer.

After the final coat of lacquer has dried, I suggest wet sanding with the grain with 600-grit, automotive, wet-or-dry paper to remove any surface defects. Afterward, you can rub out the finish to perfection using fine (0000) steel wool and mineral or paraffin oil. Check your progress frequently by wiping off an area with a soft cloth. There is the possibility of rubbing through a finish that is not completely cured. A final coat of paste wax gives more protection and a nice sheen.

There's one more possible explanation for the fisheyes. It may be that the areas where the black stain is present are sapwood, which in many species is lighter and softer than the heartwood. It's possible that the manufacturer stained these areas to match the surrounding heartwood, but they were then never finished properly. Because these parts of wood often absorb more finish and are less dense, the original finish may not have provided adequate protection against the ravages of some of the spray-on polishes so popular today. These softer portions of the wood may have been quite susceptible to silicone damage, and there is no proof that silicone washes are 100% effective against such abuse.

—TOM WISSHACK, *Galesburg, Ill., from a question by Robert L. Dean Jr., Glen Arm, Md.*

Staining Cherry, Blotch-Free

MANY PEOPLE LIKE TO USE DANISH OIL as a finish, including the pigmented versions, but may get some disappointing results on cherry, which tends to blotch.

I have a love-hate relationship with cherry myself—I love the way it machines, hate the way it finishes. As you may have noticed, cherry has a nasty tendency to blotch when stained. Even clear (natural) Danish oil finish will blotch on some cherry boards.

My home-brewed pre-stain conditioner (one cup boiled linseed oil in one quart mineral spirits) will minimize the blotching problem on cherry but won't completely eliminate it.

I flood the cherry with my pre-stain conditioner, keeping the surface wet for five to ten minutes. Then I wipe off the excess conditioner (lay the rags out flat to dry before disposing of them). I'm careful to stain within an hour or two after this treatment. Otherwise, the conditioning step will need to be repeated. Once the stain has dried, I continue with my normal finishing routine.

A completely blotch-free finish can be achieved on cherry, but it requires a different finishing technique. First I sand the raw wood to 220 grit, and then I seal the entire piece with a coat of superblond shellac (a 2-lb. cut, or 2 lb. of shellac flakes dissolved in a gallon of denatured alcohol).

Once this first coat is dry and scuff-sanded, I spray on a few coats of a 3-lb. cut of garnet lac (a darker, less-refined version of shellac) to produce that nut-brown look of aged cherry. Another sealer coat of dewaxed superblond shellac followed by two coats of waterborne lacquer complete the job.

Substituting button lac (the least refined of the generally available forms of shellac) for garnet lac will produce a darker walnut-brown. In-between shades can be made by blending the two and controlling the amount sprayed on the wood surface. Superblond shellac, garnet lac and button lac are all available from Woodworker's Supply (1108 N. Glenn Road, Casper, WY 82601; 800-645-9292).

—CHRIS MINICK, *Stillwater, Minn.,*
from a question by James Ransom, San Diego, Calif.

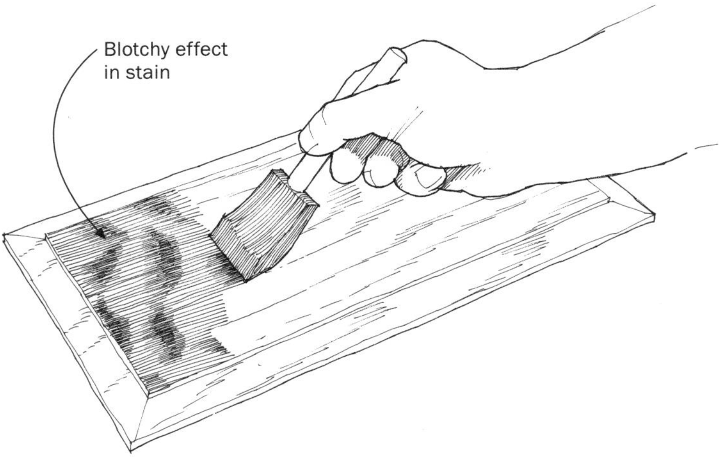

Staining Birch without Blotchiness

YOU WANTED TO MATCH the even color of commercial kitchen cabinets in your own shop. You tried a water-based stain on birch kitchen cabinets and the results were horrendous—extreme blotchiness, even when you dampened the wood and used wood conditioner. What's the difference between your finish and the commercial one?

Well, chances are good that those beautifully stained, blotch-free commercial cabinets were not stained at all, at least not in the conventional sense. The color you see on most high-end production furniture and cabinets is layered on the wood by a process known as toning and glazing. Toners can be thought of as colored finishes and are best applied with spray equipment. Glazes are generally pigmented, heavy-bodied colorants and are designed to be applied by hand.

The main difference between a toning or glazing operation and conventional staining is when the color is applied to the wood. Traditionally, staining is done on the raw wood, often with disastrous results. Applying a liquid stain directly to a blotch-prone wood like birch (cherry, pine, and soft maple are in the same category) can cause severe blotchiness.

Toning and glazing techniques avoid the problem because the color is layered onto the project after the wood has been sealed with a thin layer of protective finish. Because the color never touches the wood, blotchiness is virtually eliminated. Another benefit of coloring wood by toning or glazing is that you can precisely control the final color of the project, a particularly important feature when color-matching something new to existing furniture.

A typical toning and glazing finishing schedule is as follows:

1. Apply a coat of sealer to the raw wood. Sand to remove nibs.

If necessary, apply a ground stain (a base color) to even up color variations in the wood.

2. Apply a thin coat of sealer to lock in the ground stain.
3. Apply multiple coats of colored toners until the desired color is achieved.
4. Apply a wipe-on, wipe-off glaze to highlight the carvings, turnings, or pore structure.
5. Apply a thin sealer coat followed by at least two top coats.

Although this schedule may sound complicated, it is fairly easy to do with spray equipment or by hand.

—CHRIS MINICK, *Stillwater, Minn.,*
from a question by Hector Destefanis, Marianna, Fla.

Home-Brewed Pre-Stain Conditioner

CHERRY IS A BLOTCH-PRONE WOOD, so you need to take special precautions to minimize the problem. My home-brewed pre-stain conditioner works well with oil-based stains. To make the conditioner, mix about 1½ cups of boiled linseed oil in 1 gal. of mineral spirits. Liberally apply this mixture to the raw sanded cherry, and let it soak in for five to ten minutes, touching up dry spots as they appear. Wipe off the excess, and stain as usual.

Water-based gel stains like Smooth and Simple wood stain from Clearwater Color Co. (Highland Hardware, 1043 N. Highland Ave., Atlanta, GA 30306; 800-241-6748) also minimize the blotchiness of stained cherry. This stain is a good choice when lacquer, shellac, or a waterborne top coat is used on the project.

—CHRIS MINICK, *Stillwater, Minn.,*
from a question by Edward Jonke, Glen Arm, Md.

Evening up the Color of Cherry

IF YOU BUILD A CHERRY BEDROOM set and finish it without stain, you may end up with some objectionable stripes of white sapwood on some areas of the pieces. Regrettably, the prospects are dim that time will help mellow the sharp contrast between cherry heartwood and sapwood. The color of the heartwood in most of the darker species of cabinet woods tends to fade with time and exposure to light, but cherry is a notable exception. If the contrast changes at all over the first few years, and it most likely will, it will become substantially more pronounced.

The reason the heartwood is a different color than the sapwood is because the heartwood has been impregnated by chemicals, such as nutrients and decay inhibitors, which the living tree produces and transports along the rays for storage in the dead, interior cells of the wood. (This is true in virtually all woods.) Some of these chemical compounds are fairly complex and tend to polymerize into pigments with differing sensitivities to light, depending upon the species. While in some woods the pigments will fade when exposed to light, in others, such as cherry, light actually darkens the pigments. Since cherry's almost stark-white sapwood lacks pigment, it will simply tend to yellow a little over time, taking on the appearance of dirty ivory. The heartwood, on the other hand, will undergo the patina-building process for which cherry is well known, and shift from a pinkish-tan color to a richer and darker amber orange.

I wish I could offer a totally reliable remedy, but I don't think there is one, short of lightening the wood's natural color with very strong bleach and then staining the entire piece. Perhaps a little touch-up stain, artfully applied to just the sapwood streaks, might help make the contrast less noticeable, but it won't solve the problem entirely. Further, given cherry's perpetually changing patina, even if the match is perfect when the stain is applied, it won't stay that way.

—JON ARNO, *Schaumburg, Ill.,*
from a question by Steve Barrett, Kalispell, Mont.

Correcting Blotchy Stains

PERHAPS YOU'VE BEEN EXPERIMENTING with non-grain-raising (NGR) stains on lighter woods such as cherry. The effect is often blotchy and the colors seem to bleed. You have tried many combinations of stains, but nothing seems to help.

You should know that NGR stains are really intended for industrial users who have the proper spray equipment. They are difficult to apply by wiping or brushing. If you want to experiment a little, however, try wetting the wood with denatured alcohol just before staining. The alcohol slows down penetration of the stain and may give you better color control. If you have spray equipment, spray the stain at very low air pressure or just fog on a light coat. After the stain has dried, spray on a thin washcoat of reduced lacquer sealer (one part sealer to two or three parts thinner) or reduced shellac (one part bleached shellac to five to seven parts denatured alcohol). This will keep the NGR stain from bleeding into the top or finish coat.

—OTTO HEUER, *Waukegan, Ill.,*
from a question by Brian Shultz, Exton, Pa.

Removing Stains with Oxalic Acid and Bleach

A SCULPTOR RECENTLY COMPLETED a butternut wood sculpture and is troubled by a dark grain blemish that is visually disturbing. He would like to apply a chemical or bleach preparation to the distracting area to blend it with the adjacent area.

Unfortunately, the arsenal of bleaches we woodfinishers use is rather poor. The most important are chlorine and oxalic acid. The only way to find out how to eliminate the disturbing color in the sculpture is to experiment. Start with the oxalic acid. It is available from paint stores in crystal form and must be dissolved in alcohol. Apply the solution with a brush and allow the alcohol solvent to evaporate. You may wish to alternate the acid treatment with ordinary household bleach applied in a similar manner. When using these chemicals, beware: Use a chemical filtering mask and ventilate the area well.

If these chemicals provide no relief, you can try peroxide bleach. The peroxide may do a better job than the others, but it may also completely kill the markings of the wood. Whichever solution is used, a thorough washing with a fairly strong laundry detergent, used warm, may increase the effectiveness of the bleaches.

Finally, if all else fails, it may be necessary to camouflage the problem area under a veil of pigmented finish—in plain words, paint the desired color over the unwanted one. This requires a certain amount of skill and, surprisingly, the need for such skill frequently uncovers its existence.

—GEORGE FRANK, *South Venice, Fla., from a question by Paul S. Twichell, Keene Valley, N.Y.*

Chemicals in Cedar Ruin Nitrocellulose Lacquer

A BLANKET CHEST OF RED OAK is lined with ⅜-in.-thick tongue-and-groove aromatic cedar (commercially sold for closet lining). Several months later, the chest developed a sticky substance where the oak trim overlaps the cedar lining.

The gooey-finish problem was probably caused by gases emitted from the cedar lining of the blanket chest. Aromatic cedar contains several chemicals that are harmful to nitrocellulose-lacquer finishes. Two of these, limonene and bornyl acetate, are solvents for nitrocellulose resin but are only present in freshly cut cedar boards. However, 2-hydroxycamphene (the chemical that makes cedar smell like cedar) continues to be present in high concentrations, easily volatilizes out of the wood, and will damage nitrocellulose lacquer finishes.

Ironically, chemicals like 2-hydroxycamphene and camphor (a close relative) were used commercially as plasticizers in nitrocellulose resin in the early part of this century. A plasticizer can be thought of as a slowly evaporating solvent. They are added to lacquer formulations to increase the flexibility of the finish so that a hard resin (like nitrocellulose) is suitable for use on wood. Adding too much plasticizer causes a finish film to become sticky.

This same phenomenon happened on the blanket chest. The 2-hydroxycamphene in the cedar vaporized and was absorbed into the lacquer film. Then the chemical dissolved into the nitrocellulose resin, which over-plasticized the system and turned the finish film into a sticky mess. Therefore, nitrocellulose lacquer is not a good choice for finishing a piece that comes in contact with aromatic cedar. The gooey-finish problem is most severe when nitrocellulose-finished parts come into direct contact with the cedar liner. It would be best to redesign the chests so that there's no direct contact between the exterior wood and the cedar lining.

As far as choosing another finish, most common finishes will not create problems. Drying oils like tung oil or linseed oil, alkyd varnishes, and standard oil-modified polyurethane varnishes (such as Fletco's Varathane products) are not affected by the chemicals in cedar. However, acrylic lacquers offer what I feel is the best alternative to nitrocellulose. They can be applied with conventional spray equipment, will not yellow, and are generally not affected by the plasticizers found in cedar. Finishes composed entirely of acrylic resins are usually designed for coating metal or as all-purpose lacquers, but they'll work equally well on wood. High-quality acrylic lacquers can be purchased at stores specializing in automotive refinishing products or from your local Sherwin Williams dealer.

—CHRIS MINICK, *Stillwater, Minn.,*
from a question by Timothy B. Fields, Colorado Springs, Colo.

Aromatic Cedar Prevents Varnish from Drying

HERE'S ANOTHER PROBLEM WITH CEDAR. You used varnish to finish a cherry blanket chest. The inside of the chest and a lift-out tray were lined with cedar, which you left unfinished. A few weeks later you discovered that the underside of the lid, as well as the cherry itself, had become sticky.

Aromatic cedar contains several chemicals that are harmful to many common finishes. Among these are chemicals used for paint stripping and others that have been used as plasticizers for nitrocellulose and acrylic finishes. A plasticizer can be thought of as a slow-evaporating solvent. They are added to finish formulations to increase the flexibility of hard or brittle resins. As you might expect, too much plasticizer in the system will cause any finish film to become sticky. This is what happened to your blanket chest. One of the plasticizers (2-hydroxycamphene, the chemical that makes cedar smell like cedar) vaporized and was absorbed into the finish film, turning it into a sticky mess.

Shellac may have been a better choice for the chest because it's one of the most readily available plasticizer-resistant finishes. Plasticizer-resistant does not mean, however, plasticizer-impervious. Even shellac will become sticky when exposed to cedar vapors for a long time. Perhaps the best choice for this hostile environment would be a good-quality paste wax. Most waxes are immune to the ravages of cedar vapors but require periodic renewal to maintain that finished look. I've found when it comes to aromatic cedar, the best strategy is avoidance; I don't finish the inside at all. No finish, no problem.

—CHRIS MINICK, *Stillwater, Minn.,*
from a question by Phil Sharman, Annandale, Va.

Replacing Lacquer with Tung Oil

A CHERRY JEWELRY BOX was finished with lacquer. Unfortunately, you dropped the box in a gravel parking lot and chipped the lacquer finish. The wood wasn't dented or marred, but the lacquer has several ¼-in. or so chips. How can you repair the chip?

Getting a flawless repair will be difficult if the lacquer has been built up to a fairly substantial depth. And often, the edges of a lacquer chip are white because the finish has been fractured. Without a complete furniture touch-up kit and fairly extensive knowledge, you'd be pretty disappointed with the results.

Instead, I'd suggest refinishing the box and applying a completely different kind of finish. Personally, I don't like lacquer because to my eye it doesn't seem to "fit" the wood surface it's applied to. Strip the lacquer off the jewelry box with a good-quality paint and varnish remover, and then give it a scrub with medium steel wool and denatured alcohol. Go over it a final time with an alcohol-saturated cloth, so no trace of finish or residue is left on the wood. When it's dry, sand it with a hand-held sanding block and 320-grit sandpaper. Then follow up with 400 grit until the wood grain and color come into focus. Dust your project, and prepare for the finish.

I recommend using Formby's low-gloss tung oil. Apply a liberal coat to the entire box with a soft-bristled brush. After five minutes, remove the surplus oil with an old cotton T-shirt. Let the piece dry overnight. Subsequent coats can be applied with a wood finisher's ball, which is a piece of cotton T-shirt stuffed with cotton and tied with a rubber band (see the drawing on the facing page). Dip the ball into the tung oil, and apply a light coat to one surface at a time, with the grain of the wood. When you're done, the strokes should be feather light; no application marks should be visible. Repeat this process, with overnight drying in between, four to six times. Wait for several days after the last coat, and give the jewelry box a final rubdown. Saturate a cotton cloth with mineral oil, and sprinkle it with a small amount of rottenstone abrasive powder. Give each surface a vigorous rub along the grain. Be careful around sharp corners, or you could rub the finish. Test the surface from time to time by removing the paste from an area with a soft cloth. A satiny sheen as smooth as glass should be the result.

When the box is done, remove all traces of oil and rottenstone with soft cloths. I'm sure you'll be happy with the hand-rubbed tung-oil finish you've achieved.

—TOM WISSHACK, *Galesburg, Ill., from a question by John Kinne, Kootenai, Idaho*

Finisher's ball

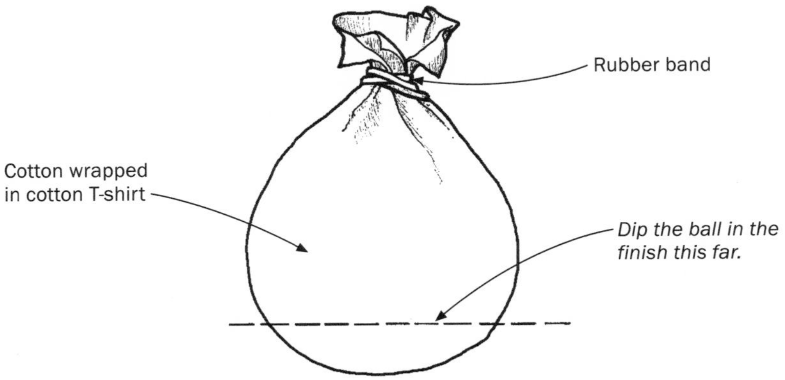

Stain Bleeding through Catalyzed Lacquer

A CATALYZED LACQUER FINISH sprayed over a dark red penetrating dye stain can have a problem. The color may come through the finish even when you've used the sealer provided by the lacquer manufacturer.

Catalyzed lacquers do present a wealth of improvements over regular lacquers, but one of their big drawbacks is their incompatibility with other finishing materials. The problem above is, unfortunately, a common one: catalyzed lacquers frequently cause severe bleeding of certain aniline dyes. I've seen one case in which an acid-catalyzed lacquer caused a particular dye color to bleed so much that the wood turned from amber to red after the lacquer was sprayed.

There is no quick fix that I know of. Some catalyzed lacquers can be recoated after they are cured, and with these finishes, the curing process sometimes "sets" the dye in the coat. In such a case, you may be able to simply respray the piece with another coat. If not, you will probably have to strip the piece and start over, which is difficult since catalyzed lacquers do not strip easily. Make certain that you test the dyes and lacquers before combining them in the future, and try switching to water-soluble anilines, which are much less susceptible to bleeding problems. Also, contact the lacquer manufacturer to see if any information on the problem is available. If the company that sold the lacquer refuses to help, it's time to switch suppliers.

—SANDOR NAGYSZALANCZY, *Santa Cruz, Calif.,*
from a question by David Goldfarb, Great Barrington, Mass.

Stain-Thirsty End Grain

When you stain a piece of wood, the end grain can absorb so much stain that it gets much darker than the rest of the piece. How can you control this so that the entire piece of wood is the same shade?

After sanding the end grain, apply a very light sealer coat before applying the stain. You can use thinned rabbit-skin glue (available from Conservation Materials Ltd., Box 2884, 340 Freeport Blvd., Sparks, NV 89431) or thinned hide glue. A very thin coat of shellac or thinned-down lacquer will also do the job. You can even apply a concoction of three spoonfuls of sugar in half a cup of water. Experiment on scrap wood first—too much sealer, and the stain won't penetrate at all.

—GEORGE FRANK, *South Venice, Fla.,*
from a question by Luke T. Welsh, Middletown, N.Y.

Lacquer-Adhesion Problem

YOU RECENTLY FINISHED BUILDING two end tables that you sprayed with lacquer for a top coat. The tabletop has a thumbnail edge with a ridge about ⅛ in. high. About a day after spraying the lacquer, cracks and bubbles began to form in the area of the ridge. Beneath the lacquer, you had used a mineral-based stain on the bare wood, followed by a coat of acrylic lacquer sealer. You stripped off the finish and sanded back to bare wood. Then you stained the tables again and sealed them with shellac before applying the lacquer sealer and top coat. The result was the same.

I suspect this finishing problem is not caused by incompatible materials but rather by an excessively thick coat of lacquer on the routed edges of the table.

When lacquer dries, two thermodynamically opposed forces are created in the film. First, surface tension gradients are formed in the still-wet lacquer as the film starts to dry. The effect of these gradients is to pull wet lacquer to the outside edge of the table, which results in excess finish along the edge. Slightly easing the sharp edges all but eliminates the problem.

Second, lacquer films dry from the top down and shrink as they dry. With excessively heavy coats, the surface dries first and then starts to shrink. Because the lacquer below is still wet, the shrinking film moves across the wet lacquer, and stress cracks are formed (see the drawing above). These cracks, known as mud cracks, widen as the film continues to dry. I think what is on the edge of the table are classic mud cracks.

A simple solution for both problems exists. Thin your nitrocellulose lacquer to between 12% and 14% solids, and spray thin coats no more than three to five mils thick. Thin coats dry very rapidly, minimizing surface tension effects and eliminating mud cracking. Multiple thin coats are always better than one or two thick ones. Experience has taught me that it is easier to spray on a few extra coats than it is to sand down a thick cracked one.

—CHRIS MINICK, *Stillwater, Minn.,*
from a question by Michael O. Goodnow, Stevensville, Md.

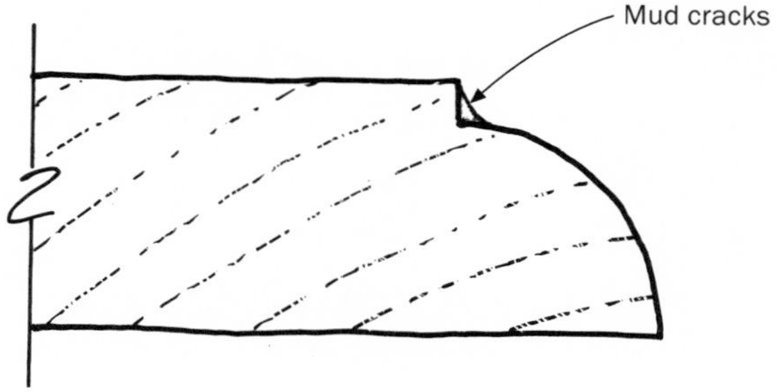

Wrinkles in Shellac Finish

AN ANTIQUE SIDEBOARD NEEDED some refinishing. After cleaning the piece with steel wool and washing it lightly with turpentine, you applied a coat of thinned-down shellac, which went on nicely and looked good. The next day you rubbed the surface slightly with steel wool, wiped it down, and applied a second coat of shellac; the finish instantly wrinkled up. Despite further cleaning and reapplication, the problem has persisted.

The most common cause for a shellac finish wrinkling is the shellac being past its viable shelf life. After shellac flakes are dissolved in alcohol, the mixture starts a gradual chemical change (esterification), which increases the flexibility of the finish but decreases its hardness. In time, the shellac will become rubbery and soft, and eventually it won't dry completely. This condition is usually not obvious on the first coat, but a second coat of material will either crack or wrinkle from the movement of the first layer. This is why it is vitally important to keep track of the age of any ready-mixed shellac finish. Only buy cans that have been dated at the factory and use up the shellac within six months of that date, not the purchase date.

Better still, mix your own shellac fresh whenever you need it. Buy dewaxed shellac flakes (available from Garrett Wade Co., 161 Avenue of the Americas, New York, NY 10013; or Woodcraft Supply, 210 Wood County Industrial Park, Parkersburg, WV 26102). These flakes have an indefinite shelf life as long as they are kept cool and dry. Add these flakes to ethanol or denatured alcohol. That way you can mix just what you need for the job and mix a new batch whenever needed.

—MICHAEL DRESDNER, *Perkasie, Pa.,*
from a question by Steve Varga, New Waterford, Ohio

Shellac's Shelf Life

FRESHLY PREPARED SHELLAC is a wonderful finishing material, one of my favorites. It sands well, seals oily woods better than most other sealers, and easily buffs to a high-gloss finish. Shellac is also one of the few materials that is compatible with both solvent-based and water-based finishes.

Unfortunately, shellac suffers from shelf-life problems. Once dissolved in ethyl alcohol, shellac undergoes a slow chemical reaction. The by-products of this reaction act as plasticizers for the shellac resin. After about six months, the concentration of by-products is so high the shellac resin will not properly dry.

Dry shellac flakes undergo a different but similar slow chemical change. This chemical reaction (called polymerization) increases the molecular weight of the resin while at the same time decreasing the resin's solubility in alcohol. Those undissolved flakes you may notice in your shellac jar result from this chemical polymerization reaction. Although this reaction is usually slow (on the order of several years at room temperature), improper processing or improper storage by the manufacturer can dramatically increase the reaction rate. Such shellac flakes are either very old or have been exposed to excessive temperatures during manufacturing. If this happens to you, I would return the remainder of the flakes to your supplier, and ask for a refund.

—CHRIS MINICK, *Stillwater, Minn.,*
from a question by Earl L. Gregory, Rising City, Neb.

Removing Milk Paint

In the process of drying, milk paint undergoes a chemical reaction, forming a resin called calcium caseinate. Calcium caseinate (the binder in some waterproof wood glues) is responsible for milk paint's tenacious adhesion, solvent resistance, and water resistance. Common solvent-based paint strippers are totally ineffective for removing old milk paint. However, highly caustic strippers like those used in automotive paint-stripping dip tanks will usually remove the paint. Unfortunately, caustic strippers often attack the wood fibers, too, turning them to a soft pulpy mess, and they are extremely dangerous. They are highly corrosive and will cause irreversible damage to eyes and skin if improperly handled. If you must chemically remove the paint from your cupboard, take it to a professional furniture refinisher who is properly equipped to handle caustic strippers and jobs of this magnitude.

Sanding the wood to remove the paint is an option that I find particularly distasteful. Sanding removes all the patina and other wear marks of age from the wood, making a valuable antique look like a reproduction.

Preserving the cupboard without removing the paint may be the best alternative. Thoroughly clean the cupboard with soap and water, and then apply a coat of Watco oil to the dried wood. This treatment will protect the remaining painted areas and preserve the authenticity of the antique cupboard. If the milk paint is badly worn, you might also consider repainting. After all, the craftsman who originally constructed the piece painted it; perhaps you should do the same.

—CHRIS MINICK, *Stillwater, Minn.,*
from a question by Stephen R. Courtner, Knoxville, Tenn.

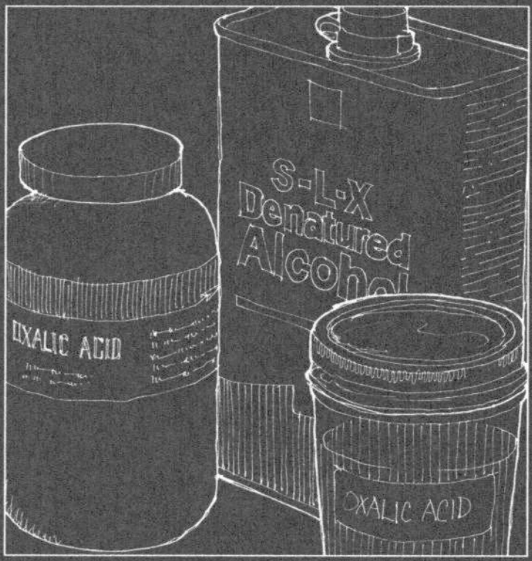
S-L-X
Denatured
Alcohol
OXALIC ACID
OXALIC ACID

Chapter 10

REPAIRING DAMAGED & OLD FINISHES

Repairing a Perfume-Damaged Finish

IF YOU SPILL PERFUME on a lacquer-finished dresser it is likely that the perfume will dull the lacquer's gloss in the area of the spill, even if the spill is removed quickly. If the finish is still intact, merely dulled by the alcohol in the perfume, you can repolish the dulled lacquer with just about any automotive polishing compound. Just follow the directions on the can's label. Be sure to buy a "polishing" compound and not a "rubbing" compound: The latter is usually a coarser grit and will not allow you to polish the finish to as high a gloss.

If the surface level of the finish in the perfume-affected area is significantly lower than that of the surrounding area, the repair will be much more difficult. The spot will require filling in some way, either by burning in with a shellac stick (if it's a very small area), respraying the area with more lacquer, or "padding in" more finish using the French polishing method. You might want to check with a professional refinisher in your area before you begin such a repair to make sure the job is not going to put you in over your head.

—MICHAEL DRESDNER, *Perkasie, Pa.,*
from a question by Richard M. Burton, Sarnia, Ont., Canada

Countering Discoloration from Alkaline Cleaning Products

WHEN ALKALINE CLEANING MATERIALS, like Windex, are spilled and left on a finish it is not unusual for them to leave a discolored spot. Chemically speaking, alkaline reacts with the natural tannic acid found in many woods to form a colored chemical complex. Oak exposed to ammonia vapors turns a pleasing brown (also called fumed oak).

Cherry treated with lye also turns brown, and sodium bicarbonate (baking soda) will turn birch gray and change blond butternut to green. Generally, woods with high tannic-acid content—like oak—produce darker stains.

To reverse the discoloration you can treat the affected area with an organic acid. Vinegar (acetic acid) isn't strong enough to do the job. Lemon juice (citric acid) is more concentrated and is a better choice. Citric acid will remove the stain if the stain is fresh and not too dark, but will not bleach the natural color from the surrounding wood. Severe stains may require an even stronger acid. Oxalic acid (available in hardware stores) almost always removes stains of this type. Unfortunately, oxalic acid may also remove the color from the adjacent wood. Try the lemon juice first. If the stain persists, you many have to use an oxalic acid wash. Prepare a dilute oxalic acid solution by dissolving one or two tablespoons of acid crystals in one pint of warm water. Wear gloves and flood the entire surface with the liquid. Keep the table wet with the acid solution for about 20 minutes. If the stain still remains, retreat the area with a more concentrated oxalic acid solution. Once the stain is gone, wash the table several times with clear water. Allow the wood to dry, then finish with Danish oil or a polyurethane varnish. A word of caution, oxalic acid is poisonous, so keep children and pets away from the work area.

—CHRIS MINICK, *Stillwater, Minn.,*
from a question by Tom Griffin, Dublin, Calif.

Removing White Water Rings

Remove the water
ring with cigarette
ashes or rottenstone.

WATER RINGS ON FINISHED SURFACES can be removed using gentle abrasives. A common method is to dab a paper towel into cigarette ashes and gently rub or scrub the white areas. It may take several rubbings and frequent renewal of the ashes to eliminate the rings. You could also use rottenstone in place of the ashes. It's available at most hardware stores and is about as gentle an abrasive as can be found.

—DON NEWELL, *Farmington, Mich.,*
from a question by Arthur B. Sayer, Morrison, Colo.

MY WIFE HAS A METHOD for removing white water rings that she has been using for more than 25 years without fail. Apply a liberal coat of Vaseline over the water ring and let it stand for a day.

The water ring will be gone and you merely have to wipe off the Vaseline. It even works on large areas, like the footboards of teenagers' beds after they leave wet towels on them.

—ROBERT J. NOETH, *Arnold, Md.*

Removing Black Water Stains from Oak

TO BLEACH OUT BLACK WATER STAINS on oak, use a 20% solution of phosphoric acid. For safety's sake, don your goggles and rubber gloves, then just brush the acid solution on the oak and put it out in the sun. Neutralize the acid after it is dry with a TSP (trisodium phosphate) or bicarbonate of soda solution. I use this procedure on old oak barrels and find it more effective than the two-step oxalic acid system sold in paint stores. The phosphoric acid also removes rust deposits from iron and steel, much the same as Naval Jelly.

—PETER S. BIRNBAUM, *Sebastopol, Calif.*

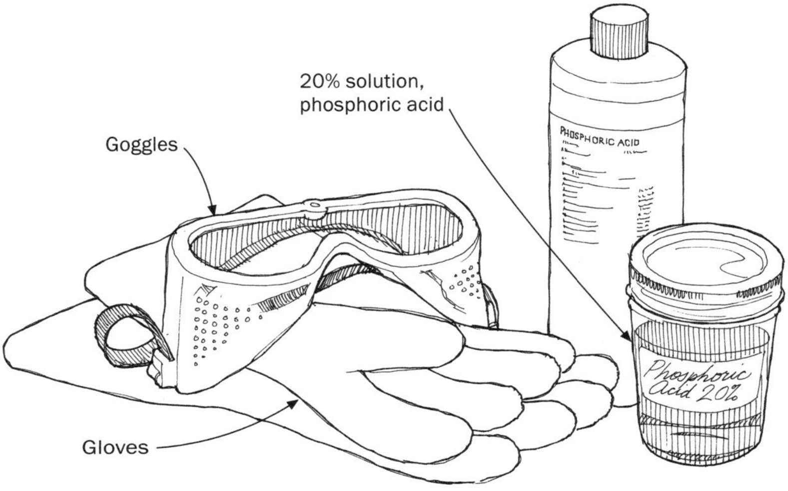

Removing Black Rain Stains from Unfinished Furniture

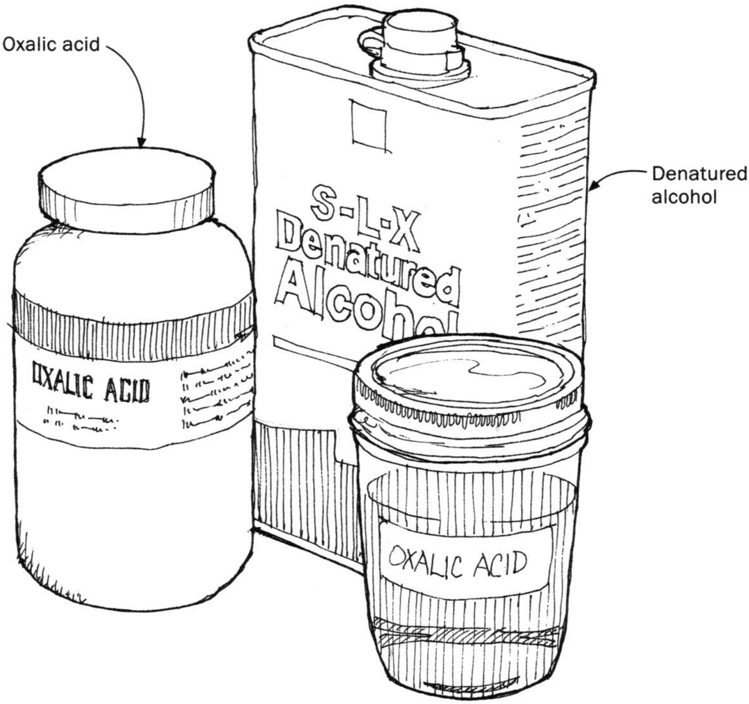

BLACK RAIN STAINS ON unfinished furniture can usually be removed with oxalic acid. Fill a small jar one-half full with oxalic acid crystals (available at some local paint supply stores and by mail from Garrett Wade, 161 Avenue of the Americas, New York, NY 10013), then add denatured alcohol until the jar is three-quarters full. Let the mixture set a day or two. Shake frequently and let the alcohol dissolve as many of the acid crystals as it can. Then apply the concentrated solution to the wood and let it set for 10 to 20 minutes. Avoid contact with metal. You may have to repeat the process to lighten the wood as much as you want. Before applying any finish, you should neutralize the acid with a solution of baking soda and water.

—GEORGE FRANK, *South Venice, Fla.,*
from a question by Harry W. Welliver, Wapwallopen, Pa.

Removing Water Stains from Teak

WATER STAINS ON FURNITURE or stereo speakers, caused by condensation on a water glass or an overwatered potted plant, are common. The cause of the stain is metallic salts in the water (usually iron) that react with chemicals naturally present in the wood to produce a color change in the wood.

Because the damage is to the wood, you need to remove the finish on the top of the speaker to treat the problem. I do not recommend stripping the finish with chemicals because it will be difficult to keep the stripper from dripping over the sides. Most speakers are finished with one or two coats of lacquer, so I find it far easier to sand the finish off. (Please wear a respirator.) Don't use a scraper, as you'll chip the veneer at the top of the edge.

When the bare wood is exposed, you can try to remove the stain with oxalic acid (available at most paint stores and in many woodworking mail-order catalogs). Oxalic acid is sold in dry crystals and must be dissolved in water. I suggest using a saturated solution, which is mixed by dissolving oxalic acid into warm water until no more crystals will dissolve. (Oxalic acid is extremely poisonous, so good woodworking practice dictates wearing gloves, a respirator, and safety glasses. And be sure to keep the solution away from kids and pets.)

Brush on enough of this solution (after taping off the rest of the speaker) to wet the wood, and let it sit for several hours. Then apply a second coat, and let the piece sit overnight. The stain should have disappeared or at least lightened. Either way, you must neutralize the oxalic acid, and remove all traces of the crystals. To neutralize the acid, make a mild alkaline solution by dissolving several tablespoons of baking soda or borax into a pint of warm water. Brush the solution on, and remove it with a dry cloth. Do this several times, and then follow up by rinsing the wood with clean distilled water (don't use tap water because it will discolor the wood again).

If the stain is gone or lightened enough, finish the top by brushing or padding on several coats of orange shellac. I find the natural orange color of shellac replaces the color pulled out of the teak by the oxalic acid. If the stain is still there, you have two options: You can re-veneer the top and finish it to match or try "painting" out the stain, using dry pigments and shellac. Re-veneering is difficult and shows up somewhat, so in my shop, we would never do it.

—JEFF JEWITT, *North Royalton, Ohio,*
from a question by I. Majer O'Sickey, Homer, N.Y.

How to Avoid Stains where Steel Meets Oak

WHEN YOU USE IRON OR STEEL FASTENERS with oak furniture, steel bed bolts for example, the oak, steel, and moisture react quickly to produce a black stain, even through a good oil or varnish finish. Red oak is particularly susceptible. The moisture can come from within the wood if it is not fully dried, or it can condense out of the atmosphere onto the bed bolts if exposed to wide temperature swings. The slightest amount of moisture will set up the reaction.

The most important thing to do is to make sure the wood you're using is thoroughly seasoned. In addition, you can set the bed bolts below the post faces, as was done traditionally on more formal beds, and cover them with brass covers. Any stains will be hidden. This will work as long as the post is thick enough not to be weakened by the holes for the bed-bolt heads.

If your posts are fairly thin or if you prefer having bed bolts that tighten on the face of the post, as was often the case on country beds, you can make some washers from medium-weight cardboard or a plastic milk jug. You could also file brass washers so they're hidden behind the bolts. All you have to do is isolate the bed bolts from the oak. If you work carefully, the washers will be all but invisible.

—GARRETT HACK, *Thetford Center, Vt., from a question by Charles Griffin, Laughlin AFB, Tex.*

Stripping Casein-Based Paint

TO STRIP CASEIN-BASED PAINT you may wish to follow Prof. Seymour Z. Lewin's approach, cited in a 1972 research paper. Lewin calls for a combination of the enzyme trypsin (available from biochemical supply houses and relatively inexpensive) and monosodium dihydrogen phosphate, dissolved in water. This solution softens casein paints and allows them to be brushed away, no matter how old the paints may be.

—JOHN GREENWALT LEE, *Annapolis, Md.*

To strip casein paint I've successfully used Bix furniture-stripping solution (Bix Manufacturing, Plumtrees Rd., Bethel, CT 06801).

—E.A. FRANKS, *Silver Lake, Ind.*

Restoring an Old Desk

HERE'S HOW I'D CLEAN UP an old water-stained walnut rolltop desk that's coated with coal dust or other serious grime. First, vacuum all of the desk parts to remove any loose dirt. Stubborn dirt and stains can be removed with a soft cloth dampened with a weak detergent and water solution. A 1% (1 g to 100 ml of water) solution of Soilax 3 works well. This product can be bought at the grocery store or a janitorial supply house. Odorless mineral spirits is another solvent for this cleanup job, but I advise against using any kind of linseed oil solution, because if it isn't entirely removed, it can remain on the surface and leave a tacky film that will attract dust and turn dark.

Glue disassembled parts with liquid hide glue, an adhesive similar to the one originally used on the desk. If you need a stronger bond, try white glue, but remember that white-glued joints are more difficult to take apart later. Rot, if not too far gone, can sometimes be hardened with several coats of a surface finish. Use a consolidant called Xylamon XL (which is available from Conservation Materials Ltd., Box 2884, Sparks, NV 89431) if you want your repair to be stronger. As a last resort, you can inject a two-part resin epoxy into any rotted areas. If the old wood is beyond repair, splice in new wood and match its color later with stains.

If the old finish remains in good condition after cleanup, protect it with a coat of carnauba wax applied with 0000 steel wool or a soft cloth. Don't apply wax to bare wood, however, because it will penetrate and be difficult to remove later if you want to apply another kind of finish. If the old finish can't be saved, try removing it with denatured alcohol or a nonflammable paint remover. Rubbing water stains with denatured alcohol may tone them down; stains can be used to match colors where patches or repairs have taken place. Shellac is probably the appropriate finish for an antique desk of this type, though it has limited resistance to heat and water. Harder finishes such as lacquer or varnish could also be used.

—GREG LANDREY, *Winterthur, Del.,*
from a question by Sam Stafford, Louisville, Ky.

Repairing a Water Spot

TO REPAIR A WATER SPOT in the beeswax polish of an old cherry serving cart, start by giving the piece a good scrubbing with 000 steel wool dipped in mineral spirits and wash away the wax, dirt, grime, and water spot. To restore the patina, make some tinted wax by melting Amber Butcher's paste wax and adding a dash of raw or burnt-umber oil color. Wax is highly flammable so be sure to do this in a double boiler so the heat source can't ignite the wax. (Keep a fire extinguisher handy and be careful.) Let the wax cool overnight.

Apply a thin, even coat of this colored wax and allow it to dry for 24 hours. Rub the wax down hard with lots of paper towels or old cotton sheets to get an even sheen. Allow to harden overnight. Repeat this colored-wax application and rubdown process at least three times. Apply a final coat of regular Amber Butcher's wax.

If there's varnish, shellac, or lacquer underneath the wax and the water spot has penetrated the finish, the repair is a little more difficult. You have to rub off a thin layer of the finish where the water spot has penetrated. First remove the wax as described above. After drying with paper towels, dip 000 steel wool into a solution of one part boiled linseed oil to one part mineral spirits. Instead of steel wool, you can make an abrasive paste by mixing rottenstone or 4F pumice with the oil solution and carefully rub it on with a soft cloth.

Rub the water spot slowly and carefully. The oil solution gives you some body and acts as a lubricant so you don't cut into the finish too quickly. This process should remove most spots and is also a good way to level minor chips in the finish. If the spot still doesn't come out it's penetrated too far and the entire finish must be removed.

After the spot has been successfully rubbed out, clean off any oil residue with mineral spirits and wipe the surface dry. Apply a thin coat of satin varnish (alkyd or urethane) diluted four parts varnish to one part mineral spirits. Tint the varnish lightly with raw umber if desired. Allow to dry for 24 hours, then carefully rub it smooth with worn 400-grit wet/dry sandpaper and follow with a wax polish. To add more color and depth you can follow the varnish coat with the colored wax process described on the facing page.

—BEAU BELAJONAS, *Camden, Maine,*
from a question by Frank W. Hollin, Philadelphia, Pa.

Cleaning an Old Finish

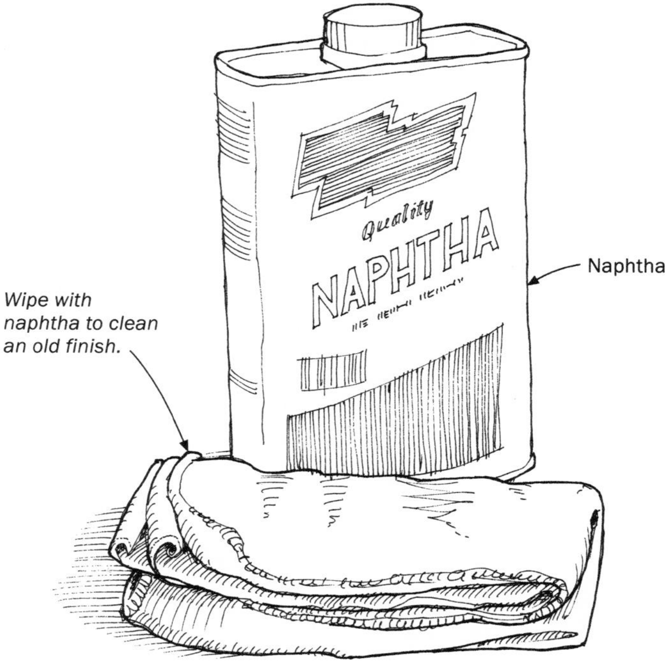

THE BEST AGENT YOU CAN USE to clean an old piece of furniture built in the 1920s is naphtha. It will effectively remove gum, tar, grease, and other built-up dirt on a finish. Most solvents will attack or soften the existing finish, whereas naphtha will simply clean all foreign matter from the surface. Naphtha will remove some of the luster of a gloss finish, but that sheen can be restored by polishing or by spraying a light top coat.

After the piece is clean, it's best to find out exactly what the old finish is before refinishing or topcoating it. If it was made in the 1920s the furniture probably has a lacquer or shellac finish. Apply some solvent to an inconspicuous place: Denatured alcohol will dissolve shellac; lacquer thinner is needed to dissolve a lacquer finish.

If it's impossible to determine what the old finish is, your safest bet is to spray a coat of vinyl sealer over the piece before applying the top coat. This sealer has platelets of vinyl suspended in a lacquer base to prohibit incompatible oils and resins from bleeding up through the layers of the finish and spoiling the new top coat. Vinyl sealer makes a compatible surface for successive coats of lacquer sealer and satin or gloss lacquer. Regardless of which top coat you use, play it safe and do a test on a small hidden area before spraying the entire piece.

—DICK BOAK, *Nazareth, Pa.,*
from a question by Kenneth E. Simon, Hatboro, Pa.

Restoring an Alligatored Finish

IT'S CERTAINLY POSSIBLE TO RESTORE an alligatored finish on an old piece of varnished furniture without stripping. We do it all the time in my conservation and restoration business.

There are two approaches you can take with an alligatored varnish finish. The easiest is simply cleaning and rewaxing the piece, which works fine if the cracks are not deep. Use a two-step method for cleaning.

First, remove all the hardware, and wipe the surface thoroughly with a cloth dampened in mineral spirits or naphtha, changing to a clean part of the cloth frequently. This will remove all oil-soluble dirt such as old waxes, polishes, and skin oils.

When the piece is dry, switch to a water-based cleaner (a capful of Dawn dishwashing detergent mixed in a quart of warm water works well). With a damp cloth, use the cleaner to remove any remaining water-soluble dirt. Finally, wipe the piece with a clean cloth.

To minimize the cracked appearance, you can sand lightly with 400-grit nonloading sandpaper. Proceed carefully, and sand just enough to knock off the surface of the old varnish. When done, clean off all sanding residue, and apply a colored paste wax that matches the overall tone of the wood. Liberon and Briwax both make colored waxes for this purpose.

If the cracks go deeper, keep sanding. Wipe the piece periodically with mineral spirits to make sure you are not sanding through any color layers. When you have removed as much of the old varnish as you can, pad on two coats of dewaxed pale shellac. I use a 2-lb. cut made from fresh flakes. When dry, rub with steel wool and wax.

An alternative product that you can use is a padding lacquer, which is shellac modified with other resins in a solvent mixture that should "bite" into the old finish. Behlen's Qualasole is a product that I have used with satisfactory results.

Although you may be well-intentioned, keep in mind that if you remove an old finish, it might destroy an antique's value.

—JEFF JEWITT, *North Royalton, Ohio,*
from a question by Robert Funk, Shelton, Conn.

INDEX